$14.07

CANADIAN
PEOPLE PATTERNS

CANADIAN
PEOPLE PATTERNS

Roger Sauvé

Western Producer Prairie Books
Saskatoon, Saskatchewan

Cover design by Robert Grey

Printed and bound in Canada

Government of Canada data used with the permission of the Minister of Supply and Services Canada, 1990.
Gallup data used with permission of Gallup Canada, Inc.

Western Producer Prairie Books is a unique publishing venture located in the middle of western Canada and owned by a group of prairie farmers who are members of Saskatchewan Wheat Pool. From the first book in 1954, a reprint of a serial originally carried in the weekly newspaper, *The Western Producer,* to the book before you now, the tradition of providing enjoyable and informative reading for all Canadians is continued.

Canadian Cataloguing in Publication Data

Sauvé, Roger

    Canadian people patterns

    ISBN 0–88833–341–2

1. Canada – Population. 2. Population forecasting – Canada. I. Title.

HB3529.S38 1990   304.6'0971   C90–097112–6

Maclean Hunter

CONTENTS

To Bonnie, Roxanne, Eric,
and the many others who have helped shape
my People Patterns.

Introduction:

A Book About Your People Patterns

There is a certain pattern to all our lives. We are born, go to school, enter the work force, form independent households, spend, save, retire, and die. Some of us may repeat certain steps or omit others as we evaluate and change and as the world shifts around us. While each of us can probably say "I did it my way," it is evident we all go through similar patterns as we progress through life.

Canadian People Patterns highlights many of the key phases we pass through during our lives. By making use of statistical information, this book examines current trends for specific age groups and income categories. It also compares trends in the male and female populations. By extrapolating from the changes observed within each of these groups over the last several years or decades, one can make predictions about the future Canadian society.

The organization of this book will enable an individual to compare his or her personal situation to that of Canadians as a group. In addition, the predictions for the future will help the reader to prepare for expected changes in such areas as educational requirements, the needs of the labour force, and changing family dynamics.

Canadian People Patterns can be used as a reference book for anyone requiring information about the makeup of Canadian society. How many double-income husband-wife families are there? Is it true that divorced people are less likely to marry than those who are single or widowed? Are incomes of older Canadians improving? These questions and their answers are not mere trivia because they deal with situations that are very important to us as individuals. "I always feel broke . . . Am I alone?" "How does my high school diploma rank compare with the educational achievements of others?" "What are the chances that I will get divorced at my age?" "What are my chances of marriage or remarriage as I get older?" "How many more years can I expect to live?" "Can the economy support me in my senior years?"

1

This is not a "how-to" book that will fix up your life. It will, however, show you the real world as measured by hard statistics collected by governments and private organizations. The examination of current trends and the projections are based on an appreciation of a real world and not on a wish list for a perfect world. This book does not attempt to give praise or place blame on people or groups for the current state of affairs . . . it just paints a picture of reality.

The information is presented in graphical and non-technical terms so that the majority of Canadians can appreciate how their world is changing. An attempt has been made to have each People Pattern stand on its own, but links between some of the People Patterns are highlighted.

The "AND SO WHAT" comments at the end of each of the People Patterns provide a condensed basis for thinking, discussing, and debating the implication of each trend. Readers are encouraged to think about their own AND SO WHATs by asking what the specific statistical trends mean for their lives now and what their likely consequences will be in the future. The closing pages look at possible futures for George and Amanda, a middle-aged man and a young woman entering adulthood.

Readers of *Canadian People Patterns* will reach at least one conclusion: our society is in a continuous state of evolution. The changes that are taking place will have an impact on us as individuals, couples, families, businesses, and governments. It is our readiness and willingness to adapt to this changing environment that will determine our place in the People Patterns of the future.

CANADIAN
PEOPLE PATTERNS

TORONTO STAR 10/3/89

Workshop explores late-motherhood myths

THE VANCOUVER SUN 19/05/89

NO KIDDING

More and more, couples are
deciding to stay childless

The Toronto Star 11/06/89

How Ottawa fails
migrant children

GLOBE & MAIL 10/3/89

Canada did well
with its immigrants

The Toronto Star, Nov. 24/89

**Declining death rate hit
undertakers' bottom line**

THE GLOBE AND MAIL, FRIDAY, JUNE 23, 1989

Men playing greater role in contraception

THE VANCOUVER SUN 1/

**THE HAPPY
HUNDREDS**

TORONTO SUN   SEPT. 19/89

The mosaic
is melting

The Leader-Post Regina, Saskatchewan Saturday, January 26, 1985

**Fewer births, fewer deaths
recorded in provincial figures**

THE MONTREAL GAZETTE   10/05/89

**More Than One in Three Canadians
Will Get Cancer Report Says**

The Basics of Population:

More Babies or More Immigrants?

Birth rate, immigration, and life expectancy are the basic elements that determine Canada's population trends. The press is filled with stories discussing these trends.

Over the last few decades, Canada has seen the number of babies born per woman fall from the highs of the 1950s and 1960s to levels far below what is needed to keep Canada's population growing into the future. A growing number of women are having fewer babies, postponing motherhood until a later stage in life, or completely giving up on the idea of having babies at all. Changing views on ideal family size, improved birth control methods, and the need for and joy of work outside the home have been key factors in establishing this trend. The current shortage of babies means that, in terms of number, our children are no longer our future.

The shortage of Canadian-born children is being filled by international migration into the country. Over the last two decades, immigrants have filled about one-quarter of the labour force expansion in Canada, and the trend will accelerate. The new immigrants are coming from areas of the world that are unfamiliar to most Canadians.

The number of years that Canadians can expect to live continues to climb, with more new beginnings filled with new relationships and adventures for the elderly.

People Pattern No. 1
Our Children Are Not Our Future

We all make choices that affect our lives; this book looks at the outcome of many of these. One of the decisions over which we have no influence is whether or not we will even be here in the first place.

In modern industrialized societies, the decision to have children is becoming very complex and is increasingly a well thought-out decision rather than an accident or inevitable fact of life. Children now have little economic value in that they no longer contribute significantly to a family's income. There was a time when children were valued as helping hands in part-time unpaid family endeavours and as a means of providing for the parents' old age. Society has in large part taken responsibility for adults with respect to income support and health care during both their working and retirement years.

For a growing number of potential parents, the "joys" of childrearing are being evaluated against the financial burden associated with raising, educating, and supporting children. In addition, more women place a high value on the "joys" of working outside the home. The joys include personal satisfaction and economic benefits. As will become evident in later People Patterns, more and more people are finding it necessary to work outside the home.

The number of unwanted pregnancies has been reduced through better birth control methods, including the pill, and easier access to abortion. As such, the decision to have children is increasingly based on economic, social, and psychological factors and less on religious beliefs or a sense that having children is the "right" thing to do.

For many years, Gallup Canada has been asking Canadians what they believe to be the ideal number of children. In 1945, 60 percent of Canadians said the ideal number was four or more. By 1985, an almost identical proportion said that two or less was ideal.

And so what . . . The growing belief that smaller is more ideal with respect to the number of children is key to Canada's future and to the forecasts presented in this book. Many forecasters are reluctant to accept the possibility of a continued downward shift in the number of children born to the typical Canadian woman. I accept the view that the downward trend will mark the future because, as we shall see, it is compatible with many of the other economic and social trends that are shaping Canada's future.

Ideal Number of Children

Despite the slight downturn in 1985, the number of people indicating two children or less as ideal has been trending upwards since 1945.

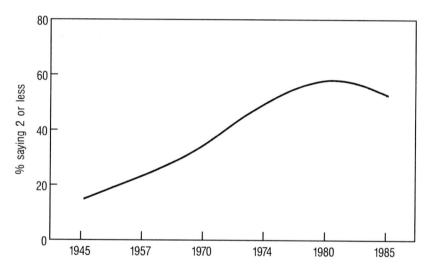

Author based on Gallup Canada Inc.

People Pattern No. 2
Not Enough Babies

At present, the average female in Canada is having less than 1.7 children during her childbearing years and this number is falling. The trend in fertility rate is plotted in the graph at the top of the next page. The average includes women who have children and those who do not.

How many children is enough? According to the statisticians, at least 2.1 children per female is needed to ensure that in the long-term, the number of births in Canada is at least equal to the number of deaths. This 2.1 assumes one male offspring, one female offspring, and an allowance for infertility and premature death.

As can be seen from the chart, the total fertility rate fell below the replacement rate during the early 1970s. Since that time, fertility has not only remained below the replacement rate but has continued to fall. The forecast outlined in this book sees the fertility rate falling to 1.2 children per woman over the next two decades. The Economic Council of Canada's 26th Annual Review has included this low fertility rate assumption in one of its forecast scenarios.

Are women merely delaying having children until they get older?

Some indicators suggest that while childbearing is being delayed for some women, it is being reduced or abandoned for an even larger number. The bottom chart expresses the number of children born per every 1000 women in specific age groups during the year. Since the early 1980s, there has been a small increase in the fertility of women aged 30–34 and 35–39. This increase has been more than offset by continued declines among younger age groups, who have and continue to have the most children. A growing proportion of new babies have no brothers or sisters. About half of all new babies born now are first children compared with about 40 percent in 1971.

And so what . . . Fewer babies means fewer adults in the future. Fewer adults means fewer people entering the labour force in later years. Fewer workers means fewer taxpayers. As will become evident, the decline in fertility will make Canada increasingly more dependent on immigration to provide the work force to support expansion in economic activity.

Total Fertility Rate

The average number of children born per woman declined from almost 4 during the baby boom to under 1.7 today.

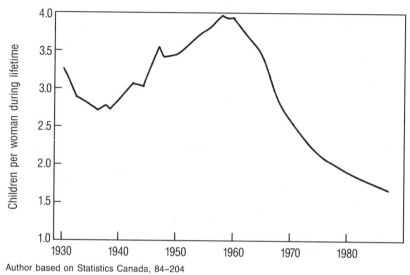

Author based on Statistics Canada, 84-204

Fertility Rate by Age

Women under the age of 30 continue to bear fewer children, while those aged 30 to 39 are having slightly more than they used to.

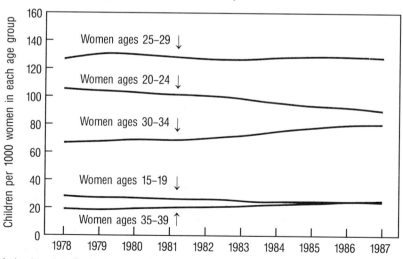

Author based on Statistics Canada, 84-204

People Pattern No. 3
Immigrants Support the Job Market

International immigration has been a key factor in sustaining economic growth in Canada. The forecast of further declines in fertility rates means that immigration will have to play an even larger role in the future to offset the actual labour force shrinkage anticipated to occur in about 20 years. Unless more immigrants are allowed into this country, Canada will be faced with a severe labour shortage in the very near future.

Presently, one out of every six Canadians was born outside Canada. Many others still hold strong links with other countries, even if their families have lived in Canada for several generations. Canada has been described as a "land of immigrants."

For three decades following World War Two, the number of international immigrants moving into Canada varied widely with peaks every 8 to 10 years. Highs of 200,000 or more were attained in 1951, 1957, 1967, and 1974. The all-time high was reached in 1957, when over 280,000 immigrants entered Canada. During the 1980s, the number of immigrants coming to Canada has averaged fewer than 120,000 per year.

The important role of immigration in supporting labour force growth is evident in the chart at the bottom of the next page. During the 1970s and 1980s, immigrants destined to enter the labour force constituted anywhere from 9 to over 100 percent of the total growth in the total Canadian labour force. Over the last two decades, about one-quarter of the total growth in the labour force was comprised of international immigrants.

The origin of persons moving to Canada has changed markedly. During the late 1960s, almost two-thirds of immigrants came from Europe. This fell to 45 percent during the mid-seventies and to less than one-quarter of total immigrants currently. The source of immigrants has shifted to Asia, which is now the source of almost half of the immigrants, and South America. In 1986, the top source of immigrants was the U.S., followed by India, Vietnam, and Hong Kong.

And so what . . . Canada, the "land of immigrants," is likely to become the "land of even more immigrants" in order to sustain labour force growth.

Are Canadians ready to see a growing number of foreigners in the job market? The immigrants will come from areas of the world which many Canadians know little about, and they will have vastly different social and cultural backgrounds. The decline in natural-born citizens suggests that Canadians will have to continue their long tradition of welcoming immigrants. People Pattern 35 points to the need for record levels of immigrants in the next century.

10

Migration to Canada

The number of people moving to Canada has been highly volatile, with an all-time high of 280,000 in 1957.

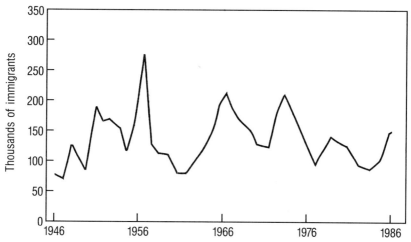

Author based on Statistics Canada, 84–001

Immigrants' Share of Labour Force Growth

Over the last two decades, immigrants have filled one out of every four new jobs in the Canadian work place.

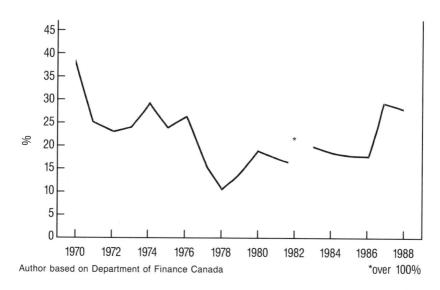

Author based on Department of Finance Canada

*over 100%

11

People Pattern No. 4

Canadians Are Living Even Longer

While we have no control regarding our birth, we do have some control over how long we will live. Canadians are choosing to live longer.

How long a person can expect to live from any age is called *life expectancy*. The most frequently used estimate of life expectancy is measured from birth. The trend in life expectancy is plotted in the graph at the top of the next page. In 1931, life expectancy from birth was 60 years for males and 62 years for females. Medical and dietary advancements have pushed life expectancy to almost 80 years for females and 73 years for males. The "most likely" population forecast discussed in People Pattern 5 sees life expectancy rising further to 84 years for females and 77 years for males by the year 2011. People Pattern 11 compares in more detail the differences between male and female life expectancy.

One of the major reasons for this significant improvement in life expectancy is the dramatic decline in infant mortality: the infant mortality rate in 1931 was 1 death per 100 births, and during the mid-eighties, the rate was estimated at 1 death per 1000 births. Infant mortality is still 20 percent higher for male babies than for female babies. It is noteworthy that infant mortality in Canada has improved each and every year since 1962.

Accidents are the leading cause of death among people aged 1–19. For the 20–44 age group, accidents decline to second place with malignant neoplasms (cancers) moving to first place as cause of death. Accidents slip to third spot for the 45–64 group and to fifth spot for those 65 and over. Heart disease is the primary cause of death for those 65 and over.

"Average" life expectancy can also be measured from different starting ages. For example, if you are now a 35-year-old woman, you can expect to live to 81 years of age "on average." If you have already managed to reach 65, your life expectancy is now over 84 years.

For men, total life expectancy is 75 years at 35 years of age and almost 80 years at 65 years of age.

And so what . . . Given the growing number of years of living remaining after retirement, individuals and society need to look at retirement as a new beginning rather than as an end. The forecasts outlined in People Pattern 8 see "empty nesters" and senior citizens forming increasing shares of the total population. The wide differentials in the ability of individuals to afford to live longer means that society may be hard-pressed to support a growing number of elderly. This problem will worsen when the number of Canadians of working age begins to decline in about 20 years as shown in People Pattern 9. Middle-aged Canadians should be planning and saving for retirement now. The anticipated labour shortage may encourage people to work longer.

Life Expectancy at Birth

Both sexes are showing continuing gains in the number of years they can expect to live.

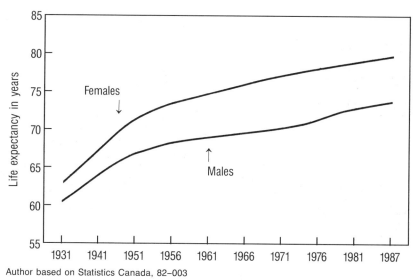

Author based on Statistics Canada, 82-003

Average Life Expectancy by Current Age

Pick your age and see how old you can expect to live "on average."

IF YOUR CURRENT AGE IS	YOU CAN EXPECT TO LIVE TO THE AGE OF	
	Males	Females
Born Today	73.0	79.7
5	73.8	80.4
10	73.9	80.5
15	74.0	80.5
20	74.3	80.7
25	74.6	80.8
30	74.9	80.9
35	75.2	81.0
40	75.5	81.2
45	75.9	81.5
50	76.5	81.9
55	77.3	82.4
60	78.4	83.2
65	79.9	84.1
70	81.8	85.4
75	84.1	86.9
80	86.9	88.9
85	90.1	91.4
90	93.7	94.5
95	97.6	97.9

Author based on Statistics Canada, 82-003, based on experience during 1985-87.

The Toronto Star 17/06/89

Elder-care programs for workers said corporate challenge of the '90s

Friday, August 16, 1985   Saskatoon, Saskatchewan   Star-Phoen

Province is 'greying'

FINANCIAL POST 24/10/88

Pension squeeze may not be as bad as feared

THE TORONTO STAR 18/5/89

Aging parents fill daughters' time, U.S. study says

THE TIMES-TRANSCRIPT 20/10/88

Statistics Canada official says Elderly population has potential to pose problems

THE MONTREAL GAZETTE   NOV. 20/89

Baby boomers to see difference in retirement

Toronto Star 24/6/89

Our Population Grew By 317,600 Over Past Year

Globe & Mail 7/6/89

Empty nest? It's crowded for parents in Toronto

Ottawa Business News, Nov. 18/89

Council Predicts Grim Future for Our Children

NEW YORK TIMES 1/2/89

CENSUS PREDICTS POPULATION DROP IN NEXT CENTURY

THE TORONTO STAR SATURDAY, APRIL 22, 1989

GROWING OLD ON A WING AND A PRAYER

GLOBE & MAIL DEC. 13/89

Population will grow until 2026, study says

Population Trends into the Future:

Grey Here, Grey There, Grey Everywhere

The "most likely" population forecast sees the number of babies born per woman declining from 1.7 today to 1.2 in the next century. A growing number of international immigrants will be needed to delay the inevitable decline in Canada's total population over the next three decades. Canada's total population will peak at slightly more than 31 million.

An unprecedented "greywave" will see the typical Canadian, who is now about 30 years old, age to about 40 in the year 2000 and to almost 50 by the year 2036. This means there will be fewer students, more empty nesters and seniors, and a shortage of workers. Young workers will have higher wages and better working conditions.

The changing age structure suggests that the social "support" system should remain strong for at least another two decades before a worsening begins and makes life more difficult for those who retire at that time.

The twenty-first century will accentuate a decline in the ratio of men over 60 to women over 60. This may further increase the odds of electing Canada's first female prime minister as women gain greater economic, political, and social power.

People Pattern No. 5

Population to Shrink,
The "Most Likely" Population Forecast

The last complete Census of Canada was conducted on June 3, 1986. The results indicated that 25,353,000 people were residents of Canada at that time. Increases of about 250,000 per year have occurred since then. Slower growth followed by an absolute decline are in Canada's future.

People who make population forecasts consider the basic and volatile trends in fertility, international migration, and life expectancy, and then make informed choices. The choices are not easy ones.

Statistics Canada has developed 17 (17 is not a typo!) possible scenarios regarding Canada's future population. Their "high" scenario assumes that fertility rates will move up again to the replacement level of 2.1 children and that 200,000 international immigrants per year will move to Canada. Their "low" scenario assumes that fertility will fall slowly to 1.2 children by the year 2011 and that international immigration will average 140,000 per year. In both cases, life expectancy is forecast to improve slowly.

I have chosen a "most likely" forecast which seems to fit best with the many underlying People Patterns presented throughout this book. Later in this book I use this "most likely" forecast as a basis for discussion. In this "most likely" forecast, the fertility rate falls gradually to 1.2 children by the year 2011. A relatively high annual international immigration of 200,000 people per year, beginning in 1996, partially compensates for the low fertility. As will be evident later, this immigration assumption is not high enough to sustain Canada's population. Once attained, these fertility and immigration conditions are maintained to the year 2036.

Using People Patterns' "most likely" scenario, the population of Canada will peak at slightly more than 31 million during the period 2021 to 2026 and will subsequently decline to about 30 million by the year 2036.

The "high" Statistics Canada scenario predicts that the population of Canada will continue to grow to the year 2036 and reach over 37 million. The "low" Statistics Canada scenario predicts that the population will peak during the 2016 to 2021 period and decline to about 27 million by the year 2036.

And so what . . . Unless war or an epidemic disease such as AIDS adversely impacts the country, the population of Canada will continue to grow, even if at a much slower rate, for at least another 30 years. Beyond 30 years, however, Canadians will likely be faced with a new reality of fewer people living within their rich geographic boundaries. The shrinkage in labour force numbers will come much sooner.

Canada's Population Forecasts

Different assumptions about the rate of childbearing and immigration lead to three population forecasts.

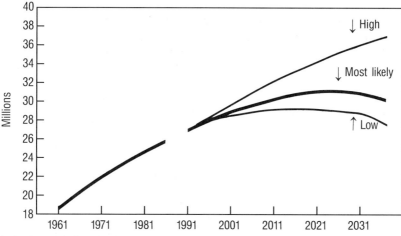

Author based on Statistics Canada

"Most Likely" Population Forecast

With a decline in childbearing to 1.2 children per woman and annual immigration of 200,000, Canada's population will peak at 31 million.

Year	Millions
1986	25.4
1991	26.7
1996	28.0
2001	29.0
2006	29.8
2011	30.4
2016	30.8
2021	31.1
2026	31.0
2031	30.7
2036	30.2

Author

People Pattern No. 6
The "Greywave" Will Transform Canada

A mighty "greywave" is coming. Within a few generations, the greywave will change Canada from a country of young people to a country of middle-aged people and in time to a country of the elderly. The impact of the irreversible trend will be enormous.

Who are the median-aged Canadians? They are those in the middle in terms of age, with half of all Canadians being younger and half being older. The median-aged Canadians are now approaching 31 years of age and have never been older.

As World War Two ended, the median age was 28 years and was at the highest level up to that time. The baby boom caused the median age to drop to a low of 25 by the mid-1960s.

As the baby boom ended and the baby bust took hold, the age structure began to rise slowly and steadily, and by the late 1970s, the median age had returned to the previous post-war peak of 28 years. The median age reached new records every year during the 1980s.

The future rate of aging will surpass any pace of aging that Canada has ever experienced. The "most likely" population scenario predicts the median age will rise to about 37 by the year 2000 and to 49 by the year 2036.

The median age of women is now about 1.5 years above the median age for men. By the year 2036, the differential will have widened to over 4 years.

Impacts of the "greywave" are already being felt. Primary and secondary schools are emptying and some of them have been converted to residences for senior citizens. The revival of 1950s and 1960s music is also a clear sign that Canadians are aging. Other impacts include a continuation of the strong growth now underway in tourism as middle-aged and older Canadians are able to take and afford expensive holidays; reduced upward mobility in the careers of many middle managers who are caught in the wave of baby boomers; and a boom in books relating to the "meaning of life."

And so what . . . The changing age structure will be the major source of challenges and opportunities facing Canadians as we enter the twenty-first century. It will affect Canadians of all ages in their personal and economic lives. This aging will force governments to take a longer view of the future to ensure that society can afford to care for the elderly and maintain the standard of living of those who have to provide the support. Marketers will have to continually adapt their programs to a rapidly aging population.

Median Age

Canada's population is older than it has ever been and the trend will set new records in the future.

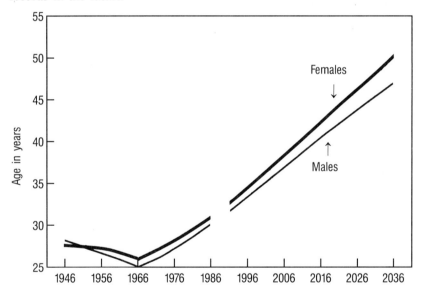

Author based on "most likely" population forecast

Fewer Students Ahead

The number of people who have traditionally formed the "potential" school age (up to 24 years old) has been declining for over a decade with no end in sight. This potential school-age group will have its share of the total population shrink further. In 1986, the school-aged base formed 38 percent of Canada's population. By the year 2036 this group will form less than 20 percent.

This potential school-age population forecast is based on the "most likely" population scenario, with an anticipated fertility rate of 1.2 by 2011 and an immigration rate of 200,000 per year.

Pre-school children (aged 0–5), many of whom will be in day-care facilities, form the basis for schools in the future. They represented almost 15 percent of the entire Canadian population in 1961 as the baby boom was in full force. This was followed by the baby bust, marked by a large number of women in their highest childbearing period fore-going or delaying pregnancy or having fewer children. This resulted in pre-schoolers constituting less than 9 percent of the total population by 1986. The number of pre-school children will continue to drop from the 2.1 million at present to about 1.5 million in 2016, and then to only 1.1 million in 2036. The declining number of pre-school children is the first direct impact of the low fertility rate of the recent past and the even lower rate assumed in the "most likely" population forecast.

The number of primary and secondary students (aged 6–16) will remain near the 4 million level into the early part of the twenty-first century. It will then begin to fall sharply over the next 30 years and dip to only 2.6 million by the year 2036. This is the second direct impact of the declining fertility rate.

The number of university/postsecondary school-aged individuals (aged 17–24) peaked at about 3.4 million in 1981 and will drop to 3.1 million in 1991 and remain at approximately this level to the year 2011. It will then plummet to only 2.2 million by the year 2036. This marks the third major impact of declining fertility.

And so what . . . The past decline in fertility has already reduced the "potential" source of students to fill the educational institutions. The evolving "baby-less" generation (1.2 children) will result in even fewer young people coming up through the system. The downward trend will accelerate further as Canada enters the next century. During the next two decades many teachers will be facing unemployment and may be leaving the profession altogether. Many school buildings may have to be closed and governments may get some relief from rising educational costs.

Potential School-Age Populations

Fewer children now means that the number of individuals of school age will decline in the future.

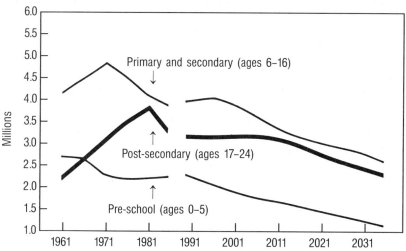

Author based on "most likely" population forecast

Detailed School-Age Populations

The number of primary and secondary school-aged children will peak during the 1990s and then decline over the next four decades.

	Number (Thousands)			Percent of Total Population		
Year	Pre-School (ages 0-5)	Primary & Secondary (ages 6-16)	University/ Post Secondary (ages 17-24)	Pre-School (ages 0-5)	Primary & Secondary (ages 6-16)	University/ Post Secondary (ages 17-24)
1986	2,181	4,008	3,407	8.6	15.8	13.4
1991	2,185	4,016	3,094	8.2	15.0	11.6
1996	2,003	4,110	3,027	7.2	14.7	10.8
2001	1,799	4,000	3,108	6.2	13.8	10.7
2006	1,654	3,676	3,182	5.6	12.3	10.7
2011	1,564	3,337	3,097	5.1	10.9	10.2
2016	1,507	3,099	2,822	4.9	10.1	9.2
2021	1,455	2,948	2,575	4.7	9.5	8.3
2026	1,363	2,843	2,414	4.4	9.2	7.8
2031	1,268	2,722	2,309	4.1	8.9	7.5
2036	1,196	2,556	2,243	4.0	8.5	7.4

Author based on "most likely" population forecast

People Pattern No. 8

Here Come the Empty Nesters and Seniors

The term "empty nester" refers to individuals or couples who no longer have children living at home. The number of empty-nesters, including people who have never had children, will increase as Canada enters the twenty-first century. The number of senior citizens will be right behind. Both concepts have already been the focus of two popular TV series. People Patterns 21 to 24 present a more detailed forecast of the future structure of Canadian households.

The long stage of having chidren, nurturing them, educating them, and then letting them go potentially begins near the age of 18 and ends at about the age of 49. The number of people in this "potential child-raising" stage is still growing quickly, but the end is near. The upward trend will end before the turn of the century with the plateau of about 14 million holding until the year 2006 and then beginning to fall gradually to under 12 million over the next 30 years. The "potential child-raising" group will fall from half of the total Canadian population now to less than 40 percent in 2036.

When the last child (or only child) leaves home the parents achieve the new status of empty nesters. They are most likely 50 to 64 years of age. This group also includes never-married singles and childless couples, who have in practice been empty nesters all their lives. According to the "most likely" population forecast, the number of empty nesters will double from just over 3.5 million now to almost 7 million during the period 2016 to 2021. At that point, empty nesters will make up over 20 percent of the total Canadian population compared with 14 percent now.

The household age group that will grow the most rapidly over the entire period to 2036 is seniors aged 65 and over. The 2.7 million currently in the seniors group will more than triple to over 8.4 million by 2036. By 2036, more than 1 out every 4 persons in Canada will be 65 or over compared with about 1 in 10 today. As this group ages the "caring" may become reversed as children look after their parents.

And so what . . . As Canada enters the twenty-first century, the decline in the number of households of "potential child-raising" age will be replaced by empty nesters and seniors. This will transform the types of homes demanded. It will encourage a move to smaller and more easily maintained accommodations for an age group with more disposable resources. Child day-care issues will be replaced by senior-care issues. Night spots, movies, TV, and physical activities will increasingly cater to older groups. There will be a greater need for health-care research into the ailments of the elderly.

Stages of Household Populations

As children leave home, a growing number of households will consist of empty nesters.

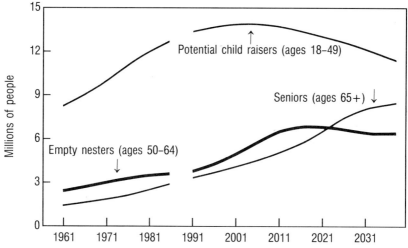

Author based on "most likely" population forecast

Detailed Household Populations

Seniors will constitute a rapidly growing share of the total population.

	Number (Thousands)			Percent of Total Population		
Year	Potential Child Raisers (ages 18–49)	Empty Nesters (ages 50–64)	Seniors (ages 65+)	Potential Child Raisers (ages 18–49)	Empty Nesters (ages 50–64)	Seniors (ages 65+)
1986	12,523	3,561	2,700	49.4	14.0	10.6
1991	13,281	3,694	3,170	49.7	13.8	11.9
1996	13,775	4,094	3,617	49.2	14.6	12.9
2001	13,941	4,878	4,001	48.0	16.8	13.8
2006	13,967	5,742	4,377	46.9	19.3	14.7
2011	13,703	6,523	4,929	45.9	21.5	16.2
2016	13,200	6,920	5,578	42.8	22.4	18.1
2021	12,871	6,909	6,561	41.5	22.3	21.1
2026	12,476	6,620	7,418	40.2	21.4	23.9
2031	11,978	6,371	8,095	39.0	20.7	26.4
2036	11,409	6,379	8,374	37.8	21.1	27.8

Author based on "most likely" population forecast

People Pattern No. 9
The "Lucky" Younger Workers

People also follow a pattern in the workplace. We typically begin at entry-level positions, move up in incomes and responsibility as we learn and mature, and then become established in work that is presumably well suited for us and that we enjoy. This section provides an overview of the potential pool of future workers. People Patterns 33 to 37 provide more specific forecasts of the labour force.

The number of individuals who could potentially take on entry-level jobs (aged 15–24) has declined during most of the 1980s and will continue to do so during most of the 1990s. A short-lived expansion at the beginning of the twenty-first century will bring the number of persons in this age group back up to 3.9 million by the year 2006. A more dramatic contraction will then bring the number of youth aged 15–24 down to 2.8 million by the year 2036. This 15–24 age group will decline from about 15 percent of the total population now to less than 10 percent in 2036. As outlined in People Pattern 40, the decline in the potential supply of younger workers has already decreased their relative rate of unemployment. The relative improvement will accelerate quickly over the next decade.

The potential number of maturing workers (aged 25–44) will reach its highest level during the 1990s as the baby boomers mature and their numbers swell to over 9 million. It will then begin a slow decline to about 7 million by the year 2036. The 25–44 age group, which is already near its peak, currently constitutes about one-third of the total population; in 1971 it constituted less than 25 percent of the total population. Many of these maturing workers are already competing for a limited number of promotion opportunities.

The pool of older workers (aged 45–64) is entering a period of rapid and sustained growth that will cause a near doubling of the number of people in this category from now until 2016. The group will make up almost 30 percent of the total population in the year 2016 compared with under 20 percent now.

The total potential labour force will begin to shrink after 2016. This points to a severe labour shortage at that time or sooner.

And so what ... The aging makeup of the potential labour force population will require new approaches by employers to attract a less flexible but more productive older work force. Younger individuals will be in a seller's market for all kinds of jobs and will surely see higher wages and better working conditions come their way. Maturing and older workers will probably have to be content with fewer promotions.

Potential Work Force Populations

The decline in number of young entry-level workers will place this group in a strong bargaining position.

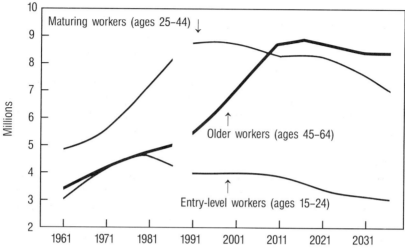

Author based on "most likely" population forecast

Detailed Work Force Populations

The number of older workers will almost double over the next 25 years.

Year	Number (Thousands)			Percent of Total Population		
	Entry Level (ages 15–24)	Maturing Workers (ages 25–44)	Older Workers (ages 45–64)	Entry Level (ages 15–24)	Maturing Workers (ages 25–44)	Older Workers (ages 45–64)
1986	4,188	8,178	4,879	16.5	32.3	19.2
1991	3,823	8,936	5,300	14.3	33.5	19.9
1996	3,781	9,104	6,109	13.5	32.5	21.8
2001	3,871	9,016	7,075	13.3	31.1	24.4
2006	3,927	8,759	8,152	13.2	29.4	27.4
2011	3,770	8,537	8,943	12.4	28.1	29.4
2016	3,432	8,550	9,115	11.1	27.7	29.6
2021	3,146	8,474	9,022	10.1	27.3	29.1
2026	2,957	8,187	8,774	9.5	26.4	28.0
2031	2,841	7,743	8,567	9.3	25.2	27.9
2036	2,750	7,221	8,580	9.1	23.9	28.4

Author based on "most likely" population forecast

People Pattern No. 10
A Lot of "Supporters" for at Least Two Decades

Our life patterns are intermingled. At certain times we are dependent on others, while at other times we must support others. Contrary to popular opinion, it seems that the numbers of "supporters" will be plentiful for at least another two decades.

A very crude measure of "dependency" is widely used to indicate the inter-relationship between different age groups. With this measure, the dependents are assumed to be the young, aged 0 to 17, and the elderly, aged 65 and over. The specific ages classified as dependents are approximate since the actual need for support varies widely, especially among the elderly.

The 18–64 age group, which is assumed to be the "supporting" population, has been growing quickly for over two decades and will continue to do so for another 15 to 20 years, peaking at about 20 million during the 2006 to 2021 period. After this period, a slow decline will lower the support group to below 18 million by the year 2036.

The number of young dependents will tend to decline continuously during the next 50-year period and will accentuate the trend of the last two decades. A low fertility rate in the past, in the present, and even lower in the future means fewer young dependents.

In contrast, the number of elderly dependents will increase throughout the period from about 2.7 million now to over 8 million by the year 2036. The greywave will hit hard (see People Pattern 6).

The decline of young dependents and the increase of elderly dependents result in the total dependency ratio continuing the decline that began in the mid-1960s. The total dependency ratio will drop to an all-time low of 49 in 2011. This means that there will be "only" 49 dependents for every 100 supporters, compared with about 57 per 100 supporters today.

Tougher slugging will begin after 2011 as the number of elderly dependents rises sharply at the same time as the number of supporters begins to drop. By 2036, the total dependency ratio will return to 70, or back to where it was during the early 1970s.

And so what . . . The low and declining total dependency ratio suggests that the support system should remain strong for at least another 20 to 30 years. The sharp increase in the dependency ratio thereafter suggests that the current support group (especially people now under 30) should be putting more money away to take care of themselves when they become the dependents because there will be fewer supporters around to help them.

Supporters and Dependents

In about 20 years, elderly dependents will outnumber young dependents for the first time.

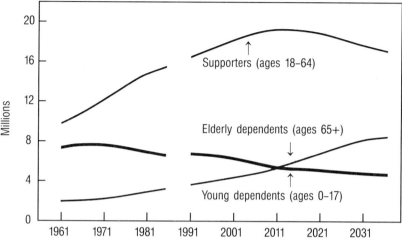

Author based on "most likely" population forecast

Dependency Ratios

The ratio of dependents compared with supporters will reach an all-time low in another two decades and then begin to climb rapidly.

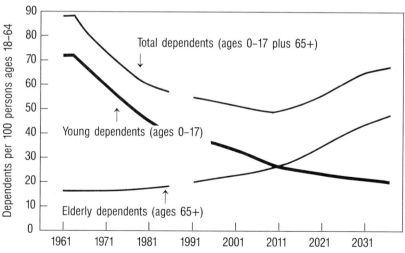

Author based on "most likely" population forecast

People Pattern No. 11
Where Have All the Men Gone?

Women have definitely become the superior sex as far as longevity is concerned, and their superiority will become even more pronounced.

A female born in 1931 could expect to live an average of 62 years, while a male could expect to live for 60 years. The difference in life expectancy in favour of females widened from 2 years in 1931, to 4.5 years in 1951, to 5.8 years in 1961, and to about 7 years from 1971 to the present. Life expectancy was examined in People Pattern 4.

The "most likely" population forecast used in this book sees life expectancy rising to 84 for females and 77 for males by the year 2011. The forecast assumes that life expectancy will stabilize after 2011.

This differential change in longevity has caused the total number of females to increase relative to the total number of males. In 1961 there were only 98 females per 100 males. By 1971, equality of numbers was attained and by 1986 there were already 103 females for every 100 males in Canada. This differential is projected to rise to 110 females per 100 males by the year 2036.

Because the differential is caused by females outliving males, the number of females would outnumber the number of males even more if male births did not exceed female births.

According to the "most likely" population forecast, there will be 105 females for every male in 2001. The projected number of women will be less than the number of men up to the 30–39 age group, after which the ratio advances quickly in favour of the women. For those between the ages of 60 and 69, there will be 111 women for every 100 men, rising to 134 for the 70–79 age group, to almost 200 for the 80–89 age group, and to over 300 for those aged 90 and over.

And so what . . . The growing "shortage" of men, especially among individuals aged 60 and over, may lead to different housing needs as more women either live alone or share accommodations with other women. Social and travel activities where both older men and women meet will become more dominated by women. Older single women will have to become even more aggressive in the dating game. Successful female politicians should tend to grow in relative terms and increase the chances of electing Canada's first female prime minister.

Ratio of Women to Men

Women will find that they increasingly outnumber men in Canada.

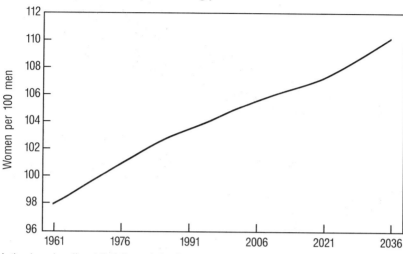

Author based on "most likely" population forecast

Ratio of Women to Men by Age Group

After the age of 40, women are more and more likely to outnumber men.

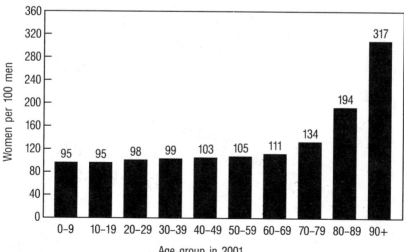

Author based on "most likely" population forecast

29

WEDNESDAY, JANUARY 10, 1990 SASKATOON, SASKATCHEWAN STAR PHOENIX

Schools face enormous social, economic changes

THE CHRONICLE HERALD 27/4/89

Greater effort said needed to reduce illiteracy rate

THE OTTAWA SUN 22/06/89

School: Key to survival

The Leader-Post Regina Mon., Dec. 15, 1986

University grads make more money

CANADA NEWS 3/2/89

PhDs rise in Canada

FINANCIAL TIMES DEC. 25/89

Family income figures prove that a university degree does pay

The Globe and Mail 10/05/89

Report urges more spending on job training

CANADA NEWS 24/3/89

Mom and Dad are back at school

Vancouver Province 07/05/89

Tough to be student

STAR PHOENIX SEPT. 28/84

University Degree Aids Earning Potential

The Education Payoff:

Go to School and Rake in the Money

Individual Canadians and Canadian society as a whole see education as a key factor in personal and national well-being.

The level of formal schooling received by Canadians has been rising over the entire post-war period, with both the general population and the labour force making substantial academic gains.

This formal education is being supplemented by courses taken on a part-time basis. More than one in five adult Canadians take courses relating to jobs, hobbies, and personal development. Adult education courses are helping to sustain enrollment at universities and colleges in the face of a declining number of younger individuals, who make up the more traditional attendees at such institutions. Those with more years of formal schooling are also the ones who are taking adult courses.

The rewards of education are undeniable. Higher education means more job opportunities, better paying jobs, and less chance of being unemployed. A university degree adds many thousands of dollars to the annual incomes of middle-aged working Canadians. Higher education is also helping to reduce women's disadvantage in earning power, although much progress remains to be made.

People Pattern No. 12

Going to School Longer

The number of years of formal education received by Canadians has risen for many years. The trend will certainly continue.

The median number (half have more education and half have less) of years of formal schooling reached 12.2 years in 1986, compared with 10.6 years in 1971. This steady improvement is equal to about 1 percent per year and is responsible for much of the increase in productivity of the Canadian economy.

Younger generations of Canadians have consistently gone to school longer than their parents. The 1986 Census of Canada found that the median number of years of schooling for the generation aged 75 and over was 8.8 years, for the generation aged 45–54 it was 11.4 years, and for the generation aged 25–34 it was 12.9 years.

Another measure of educational achievement is the highest level of schooling attained by the total population aged 25 and over. More people are now in the higher categories. In 1951, the highest level of schooling for the majority of Canadians was eight years or less. By 1971 this was down to 40 percent, and by 1986, those with only grade eight or less were down to 20 percent. This decline signifies that more people are continuing their education into high school and university.

Since 1971, about 38 percent of the total population aged 25 years or older has had all or some secondary schooling (grades 9–13). In 1986, 11 percent of all persons aged 25 and over had a university degree.

Both men and women have about 12.2 years of formal schooling, but only 8.8 percent of females have a university degree compared with 13.5 percent for males.

And so what . . . Rising educational levels are and will continue to be a prime mover for personal development and for the total economy. The changing age structure of the total population (see People Pattern 6) should tend to reduce overall demands on the educational system. Older Canadians will be encouraged to continue or to return to school. If not, some universities may close during the twenty-first century.

Formal Schooling

Increases in formal schooling have improved the productivity of the economy.

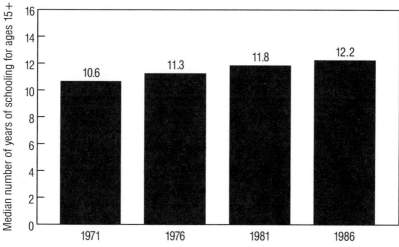

Author based on Statistics Canada, Census of Canada

Highest Level of Schooling

Nineteen-eighty-one was the first year that the number of people with at least some post-secondary education surpassed the number with grade 8 or less.

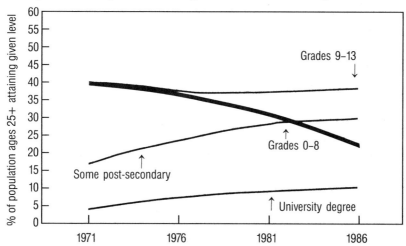

Author based on Statistics Canada, Census of Canada

People Pattern No. 13
Adult Education Is Cool

Many people continue their education on a part-time basis in public schools, private or commercial schools, and in non-school settings such as the workplace, churches, and voluntary organizations.

A government survey of 46,000 individuals taken during 1984 found that about 21 percent of all adult women in Canada participated in adult continuing education. For adult men, the rate of participation was lower, at 17 percent. This ratio excludes adults who attended school full-time.

Participation in adult education classes varies significantly by age. Those most likely to take classes are men and women aged 25 to 44. After the age of 45 participation drops off sharply.

Women are more likely to take personal development and hobby-related courses (56 percent of all courses taken by women), while men are more likely to take job-related courses (57 percent of all courses taken by men). The table at the bottom of the next page suggests that women have a more balanced approach to continuing education throughout their lives, with courses fairly equally distributed among the three categories. The percentage of divorced, separated, and single women who take job-related courses is higher than it is for married women.

Over 80 percent of both men and women who take job-related courses do so to improve their employment opportunities. About 56 percent of the job-related courses taken by men are paid for by the employers, compared with 44 percent for women.

The survey found that the higher the level of formal education an individual already has, the more likely that individual is to pursue part-time education.

And so what . . . The age-specific nature of continuing education suggests that the demand for courses will continue to be strong for a few more decades before declining. The more rapid pace of change in the job market, coupled with more working women, will see job-related courses become more popular. Personal development courses will also see increased demand.

Participation in Continuing Education

People 25–44 years old are most likely to be taking adult courses.

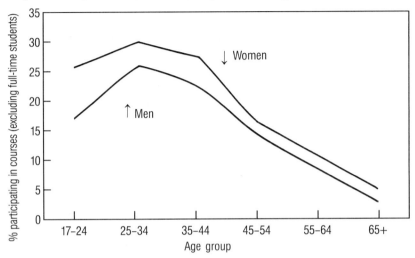

Author based on Secretary of State, S2–139/1984

Top Three Types of Continuing Education Courses

Men are more likely than women to take job-related courses.

Age Group	Men		Women	
	Top Three Types of Courses	% of Courses Taken	Top Three Types of Courses	% of Courses Taken
17–24	Job-related	54	Job-related	30
	Academic	22	Hobby	23
	Personal Development	14	Personal Development	23
25–34	Job-related	57	Job-related	29
	Personal Development	17	Hobby	28
	Academic	15	Personal Development	26
35–44	Job-related	61	Job-related	31
	Personal Development	19	Personal Development	30
	Hobby	9	Hobby	24
45–54	Job-related	64	Hobby	31
	Personal Development	17	Job-related	29
	Hobby	10	Personal Development	28
55–64	Job-related	50	Hobby	37
	Personal Development	24	Personal Development	32
	Hobby	16	Job-related	24

Author based on Secretary of State, S2–139/1984

People Pattern No. 14

A Better Educated Work Force

The last decade has seen a major advance in the educational achievements of the Canadian labour force. The improvement is evident for men and women in all age groups.

The measurement of educational levels presented here differs from the previous two People Patterns in that only those individuals who are actually in the labour market are included. Educational levels of those in the labour force are generally higher than for the total population.

Within the total labour force, the percentage of individuals that have only zero to eight years of education fell from 16.9 percent of the labour force in 1979 to 9.3 percent in 1989, or by 7.6 percentage points. The percentage of the labour force with all or part of a secondary school education fell from being the clear majority of the work force in 1979 to being just a bit less than the majority in 1989.

Each of the other three categories presented in the table on the opposite page increased as a proportion of the total labour force. The most rapid advance has been for holders of postsecondary certificates or diplomas; their numbers rose to 16.3 percent of the labour force in 1989. The advance for university degrees was right behind.

Women have made big improvements, with the percentage of women with a university degree advancing at a faster pace than is the case for men. In 1979, 8.6 percent of women in the labour force had earned a university degree; by 1989, this had risen to 14 percent.

The improvement in the educational standards of the labour force is evident both for 15–24 year olds and for the 25 and over group.

And so what... The trend to higher education is unrelenting as is evident in the dramatic strides achieved during the last decade. We all know that education is the biggest step towards personal and national prosperity. The rapidly changing use and mobility of technology, money, and people on a worldwide basis means that the educational institutions will have to be more adaptable than in the past in terms of both course content and teaching staff.

Educational Levels of Labour Force

Female university graduates in the labour force jumped from 8.6 percent in 1979 to 14 percent in 1989.

	0-8 Years School (%)	All or Part of Secondary School (%)	Some Post-Secondary (%)	Post-Secondary Certificate/ Diploma (%)	University Degree (%)
TOTAL					
1979	16.9	53.7	8.1	10.9	10.3
1989	9.3	49.0	10.5	16.3	14.9
Change 1979-1989	−7.6	−4.7	+2.4	+5.4	+4.6
Men					
1979	19.7	51.5	8.0	9.3	11.4
1989	11.3	48.6	10.0	14.4	15.7
Change 1979-1989	−8.4	−2.9	+2.0	+5.1	+4.3
Women					
1979	12.6	56.9	8.2	13.6	8.6
1989	6.9	49.4	11.1	18.6	14.0
Change 1979-1989	−5.7	−7.5	+2.9	+5.0	+5.4
Men and Women 15-24					
1979	5.6	70.2	11.5	8.8	3.9
1989	4.1	60.5	17.4	13.0	5.0
Change 1979-1989	−1.5	−9.7	+5.9	+4.2	+1.1
Men and Women 25+					
1979	21.0	47.6	6.9	11.8	12.7
1989	10.6	46.1	8.8	17.1	17.4
Change 1979-1989	−10.4	−1.5	+1.9	+5.3	+4.7

Author based on Statistics Canada, 71–529

People Pattern No. 15
More Education Equals More Income

Don't believe all those hard luck stories of PhD graduates driving taxis and MBA graduates without jobs five years out of school. They are clearly exceptions. Education has a big payoff for most of us. Higher education definitely means more jobs, less unemployment, and more money for the better educated.

According to data derived from the 1986 census, unemployment rates drop sharply as the level of education increases. In that year, people with zero to eight years of education had an unemployment rate of 14.6 percent, and people with a university degree had an unemployment rate of 5.5 percent. The most significant decline in unemployment rates occurs with the possession of a high school diploma.

Higher education not only leads to lower unemployment but also to higher participation in the labour force and higher incomes. When compared with those with less education, a university degree adds at least $12,000 to the annual income of a man aged 25–44, and at least $9,000 to the annual income of a woman aged 25–44. The advantage is even greater among older workers.

Higher levels of education seem to open relatively more doors for women. While the rates of participation in the labour force rise in line with levels of education for both sexes, participation rates rise more quickly for women. In 1986, women with zero to eight years of education had a participation rate of 37.4 percent, compared with 73.4 percent for men with the same number of years of education. This is a difference of 36 percentage points. The participation rate for women with a university degree was 84.6 percent, and the rate for men was 95.2 percent. This is a difference of 10.6 percentage points.

In 1986, women working full-time for a full year earned less than men at all educational levels, but the differential tended to narrow as education levels rose. A 25 to 44-year-old woman with a university degree received 72 percent of a man's income. A woman with zero to eight years of education received 60 percent of a man's income.

Another interesting feature of income comparisons based on sex is that the women's disadvantage is smallest among younger workers at each educational level. Income comparisons are highlighted again in People Pattern 45.

And so what . . . Personal and public funds allocated to education have a very measurable positive payoff. The payoff is so significant that it is extremely important that higher education continues to be available to all income groups and to all age groups. Upgrading of skills among older workers should receive a much higher priority.

Unemployment by Level of Education

Higher education reduces the likelihood of being unemployed.

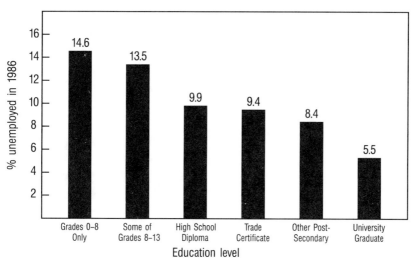

Author based on Statistics Canada, 1986 Census

Labour Force Characteristics by Level of Education

In 1986, a man between the ages of 45 and 64 with a university degree earned about $56,000 compared with about $33,000 for a man in the same age range with a high school diploma.

	Grades 0-8 Only	Grades 9-13 Without Graducation	Secondary School Graduation	Trade Certificate	Non-University Post Secondary	University Degree
MEN						
Labour Force Participation %	73.4	76.0	88.5	91.6	94.5	95.2
Unemployment Rate %	14.0	12.9	9.0	8.5	8.0	4.5
Average Employment Income $ (Full-time, Full-year)						
Ages 15–24	14,096	16,047	16,812	17,379	18,874	20,621
Ages 25–44	22,943	25,724	27,745	28,893	29,719	41,340
Ages 45–64	24,124	29,158	33,404	31,962	33,164	55,761
WOMEN						
Labour Force Participation %	37.4	52.7	68.4	74.5	78.7	84.6
Unemployment Rate %	15.8	14.4	10.9	11.4	9.0	7.0
Average Employment Income $ (Full-time, Full-year)						
Ages 15–24	10,244	12,389	13,454	12,723	15,159	18,404
Ages 25–44	13,830	16,812	18,743	18,220	20,509	29,919
Ages 45–64	14,564	17,574	19,682	20,062	21,493	35,202

Author based on Statistics Canada, 1986 Census

Survey shows state of marriage

MARKETING 26/09/88

Here come the stat on love and marriag

Chatelaine May 1989

Husband material for the '90s: what's in, what's out

THE VANCOUVER SUN, OCT. 30/87

Catering
to
SINGLES

GLOBE & MAIL 2/4/89

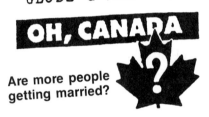

OH, CANADA?

Are more people getting married?

TORONTO STAR 02/10/88

8% of Canadian couple aren't married, agency sa

TORONTO STAR 22/1/89

Aftershocks of divorce still echo after a decade

HINTON PARKLANDER 03/27/89

THE CLARION 7/2/89

Undoing the knot

Ties of marriage increasingly loose nationwide

Marriage and Divorce:

Getting Together, Coming Apart, and Doing It Again

The press stories tell us about the changing patterns of marriage and divorce in Canadian society.

Young couples are delaying marriage like never before with both brides and grooms getting married later in life. A growing proportion of people are chosing to live as singles.

The practice of living together outside the formal bonds of matrimony is growing more significant with each passing generation and reflects a society where the needs of the individual are likely increasing relative to the desires of parents and religion. Close to one-third of young couples 25 years of age and under are living in a common-law relationship.

"Till divorce do us part" is becoming the reality for more and more couples. The chance of divorce for couples under the age of 20 is about 40 percent and declines slowly with age. The number of divorces has grown rapidly throughout the last decade, emphasizing the need for schools to teach both family and divorce law.

For those above the age of 25, the chance of getting married or remarried is highest for those who are divorced, followed by the widowed, and then the never married.

People Pattern No. 16
Putting Off Marriage

Legal marriage is still the preferred lifestyle for the majority of adult Canadians. Even so, legal marriage is happening later and a growing percentage of adults are not marrying at all.

The latest information suggests that 14 percent of women and 17 percent of men will never marry. For both sexes, the proportion who will never marry has risen by about 6 to 7 percentage points since the early 1970s.

Those who are "tying the knot" for the first time in a legal marriage are increasingly delaying the event. In the early 1970s, the median age of a first-time bride was 22.5 years; now the median age has risen to almost 25. During the same time period, the median age of a first-time groom has risen from just under 25 years to about 27 years.

The age difference between first-time brides and first-time grooms is narrowing very slowly. In 1988, the groom was 1.9 years older than the bride; in 1971 he was 2.3 years older than his bride.

This gradual delay for first-time legal marriages reflects the growing tendency for couples to live together for some time before getting legally married. It also reflects women's growing financial independence.

The total number of marriages (first and subsequent) has declined erratically over time. During the last half of the 1980s, the number of marriages has been lower than at any time during the 1970s and early 1980s. The number of first-time marriages was down to fewer than 140,000 in 1987; there were over 170,000 first-time marriages during the early 1970s. A growing proportion of the brides and grooms have been married before.

And so what . . . The larger proportion of people who are choosing to remain single, combined with the delay in marriages for those who legally marry, points to a further reduction in fertility over the long term. Caterers, clothiers, florists, and photographers will need to look beyond weddings and kids' birthdays to find business.

Age at First Marriage

The age difference between grooms and brides has been reduced from 2.3 years in 1971 to 1.9 years in 1988.

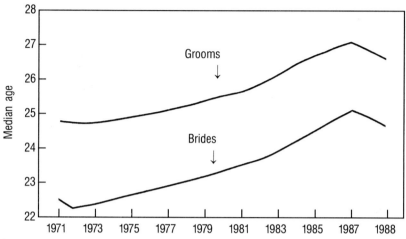

Author based on Statistics Canada, 84–205

Number of Marriages

The number of marriages was much lower in the 1980s than in the 1970s.

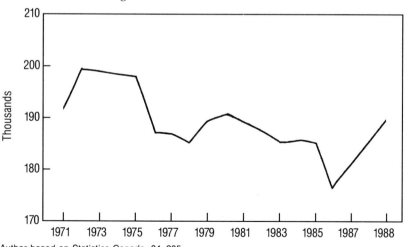

Author based on Statistics Canada, 84–205

People Pattern No. 17
"Living Together" Now a Fact of Life

Young couples are still forming "first unions" as early as their parents and grandparents did. The delay in legal marriages is being offset by a dramatic increase in cohabitation or common-law relationships.

The 1960s were filled with media debate on the demise of marriage and its replacement by "living together." In spite of this, it took almost 25 years for public agencies to collect and analyze data on the number of "non-legal" couples.

In 1984, Statistics Canada asked a large sample of Canadians a very specific and personal question: "Have you ever been a partner in a common-law relationship? By this we mean, partners living together as man and wife, without being legally married." The question asked was direct enough that it ruled out "brief casual episodes of cohabitation" or "one-nighters."

The 1984 survey found that less than 2 percent of women aged 40–59 who reported that they had formed their first union by the age of 25 claimed that it had been a common-law relationship. Among women aged 30–39, a larger 13 percent reported that their first union had been a common-law relationship. An even larger 30 percent of women aged 18–29 stated that their first union had been a common-law relationship. For men the pattern was similar, with younger generations much more prone to forming common-law unions as a first union.

The following charts suggest that women are forming first unions as early as in the past and that men are actually forming first unions earlier than in the past, but in both cases they are increasingly of a common-law type. By age 25, 70 to 75 percent of women in each generation had formed a "first union" and 50 to 64 percent of men had done so. Among the older groups most first unions were legal marriages, while for the 18–29 age group roughly one-third of first unions were common-law or cohabitation relationships.

The 1984 survey also concluded that within a 15-year period, a common-law union has roughly a 54 percent chance of becoming a legal marriage, a 12 percent chance of remaining as a common-law relationship, and a 34 percent chance of dissolving. As will be seen in the next People Pattern, the dissolution rate is about the same as for someone who married by the age of 25.

And so what . . . The existence and acceptance of meaningful couple relationships outside of legal marriage is a reflection of a rapidly evolving society in which the needs of individuals seem to be replacing more traditional values.

"First Unions" of Women by Age 25

While the likelihood of having formed a first union by age 25 is similar for each of the four generations, women in younger age groups are more likely to have begun with a common-law relationship.

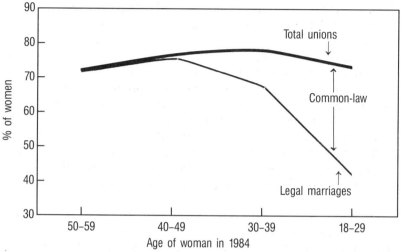

Author based on Statistics Canada, 99–953

"First Unions" of Men by Age 25

A younger generation of men are forming significant relationships earlier than their elders, even if fewer are becoming legally married.

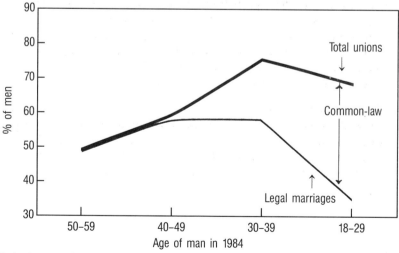

Author based on Statistics Canada, 99–953

People Pattern No. 18
Chances of Divorce Rising

Divorce used to be a rare event in Canada. Today about 3 out of 10 marriages end in divorce, and the rate is rising. "Till divorce do us part" is a growing trend.

The number of divorces granted over the last two decades has increased steadily, except for a slow decline between 1982 to 1985. Between 1985 to 1987, the divorce rate again rapidly increased to reach record highs. About 87,000 divorces were granted in 1988. This compares with 188,000 legal marriages.

A sophisticated model developed by Statistics Canada calculates the probability of divorce at various ages based on the actual experience during the 1984 to 1986 period. The model does not differentiate between first or subsequent marriages or how long a person has been married.

The chart opposite suggests that young people who are currently married and are aged 20 years or less have a roughly 40 percent chance of divorce before they reach the age of 80. At age 25, the chance of divorce is about 35 percent for wives and even higher for husbands.

The likelihood of divorce declines with age. A 30-year-old husband has a 33 percent chance of divorce, a 40-year-old husband has a 20 percent chance, and a 50-year-old husband a 10 percent chance of divorce before the age of 80. A 70-year-old man has a slim 1 percent chance of divorce. The probability of divorce is lower for women at all ages because they are more likely to be widowed.

On average, men divorce at 42 years of age, and women at 39 years. The average man remains divorced for 8.3 years, and the average woman remains divorced for almost 16 years. In either case, the divorce could end by remarriage or death.

And so what . . . The high likelihood of divorce suggests that newlyweds and those in long-term marriages may increasingly turn to marriage contracts to protect themselves in case of divorce. Pension and benefit plans will increasingly need to anticipate the repercussions of a future divorce. Schools should teach family law.

Number of Divorces

Divorces have risen to record levels in recent years.

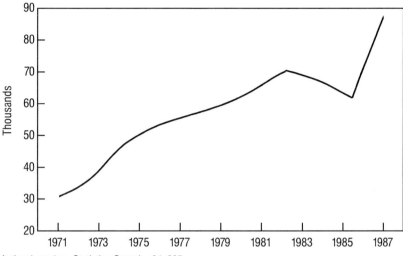

Author based on Statistics Canada, 84–205

Likelihood of Divorce

Husbands aged thirty have a 33 percent chance of divorce before they are 80, compared with 29 percent for wives of a similar age.

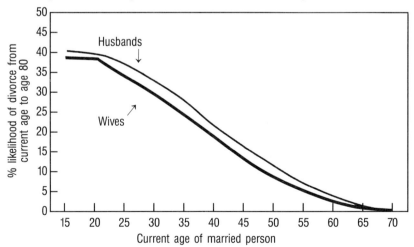

Author based on Statistics Canada, 84–536, and experience during 1984 to 1986 period

People Pattern No. 19
Chances of Marriage or Remarriage

Many single, divorced, and widowed people want to get married. The odds that they will ever do so varies significantly depending on their current age and marital status. In this section, the term *marriage* refers to legal marriages only.

The charts on the opposite page present the chances of marriage or remarriage at different stages in life. For both men and women, the probability of marriage declines significantly with age.

For men and women at all ages, the currently divorced have the highest chance or likelihood of getting married or remarried before the age of 80, followed at most ages by the widowed, and then by single never-married persons. The expression "Once bitten twice shy" does not seem to fit the real world.

The chance of marriage for single never-married women drops from over 85 percent at age 20, to 75 percent at age 25, to about 50 percent at age 30, to 33 percent at age 35, and down to about 20 percent by the age of 40. For a 40-year-old divorced woman, the chances of remarriage are higher at 62 percent, while for a 40-year-old widow the probability of remarriage is at 37 percent.

The chance of marriage for single never-married men drops more slowly, from over 85 percent at age 20, to 80 percent at age 25, to about 65 percent at age 30, to 45 percent at age 35, and to 20 percent at age 40. Widowed and divorced men still have at least an 80 percent chance of remarriage up until the age of 40.

The differing chances of remarriage between men and women mirrors the shorter time that a man spends in a divorced state (8.3 years) compared with a woman (15.8 years). A similar male-female differential with respect to remarriage exists for widowed people.

And so what . . . The high incidence of remarriage for the divorced and widowed suggests that the desire for companionship and intimacy remains a major drive. Canadians still want to learn the secrets of a happy, if not permanent, marriage.

Likelihood of Marriage for Men

At every age, divorced or widowed men are more likely to marry than are men who have never been married.

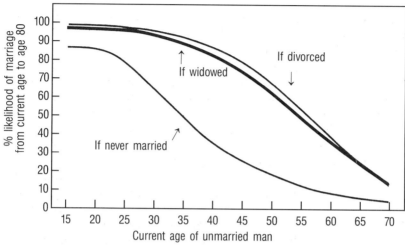

Author based on Statistics Canada, 84–536, and on experience during 1984 to 1986 period
Note: Excludes common-law unions.

Likelihood of Marriage for Women

Divorced women are more likely to remarry than are women who are widowed.

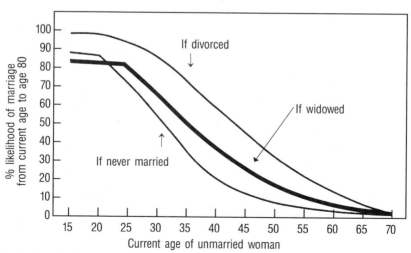

Author based on Statistics Canada, 84–536, and on experience during 1984 to 1986 period
Note: Excludes common-law unions.

People Pattern No. 20
Down the Aisle Again

There was a time when a wedding joined up two relatively young people who were making the trip for the first time. Today, the couples come in many other combinations.

In 1950, over 90 percent of the brides and grooms were walking up the aisle for the first time. Most of the rest were widows or widowers.

The proportion of all marriages comprised of first-time brides and grooms declined to below 90 percent during the late 1970s, fell to below 80 percent during the early 1980s, and is now nearing 75 percent.

Not unexpectedly, the percentage of widows and widowers among remarriages has remained fairly constant, within a 3 to 5 percent range.

The most rapid increase in marriages has been by individuals who are currently divorced. In 1971, about 8 percent of brides and grooms had been divorced. Today, people who were previously divorced account for over 20 percent of all brides and grooms. In addition, a growing proportion are walking up the aisle after having lived together in a common-law relationship (see People Pattern 17).

Remarriage as a proportion of total marriages rises with the age of the bride and groom. In 1987, only 3 percent of the brides aged 20–24 had been married before, while 16 percent of the brides aged 25–29 had been previously married, 46 percent of those aged 30–34 had been previously married, and over 80 percent of all brides married after the age of 45 had been previously married.

In 1987, the number of remarriages of brides aged 32 surpassed the number of first-time marriages of brides that age. The pattern for grooms was similar, with the number of remarriages surpassing the number of first-time marriages by the age of 34.

And so what . . . Remarriages pose questions regarding the etiquette to be followed regarding dress, gifts, and whose parents should foot the bill (or is it the couples themselves?). In any case, the "shoulds" are not as important as they used to be. Remarriages are blurring the traditional links within the home unit and between relatives. Blended families lead to multiple grandparents (and perhaps more gifts) and multiple parents or step-parents. Households with several family names are becoming more common.

Previous Status of Brides

A growing proportion of brides have been married before.

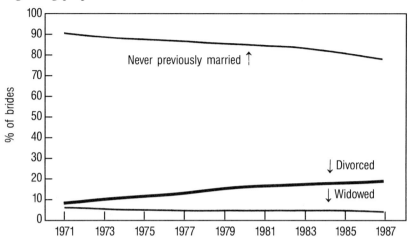

Author based on Statistics Canada, 84–205
Note: Legal marriages only.

Remarriages as Share of Total Marriages

In 1987, the majority of brides and grooms in their thirties or older had been married before.

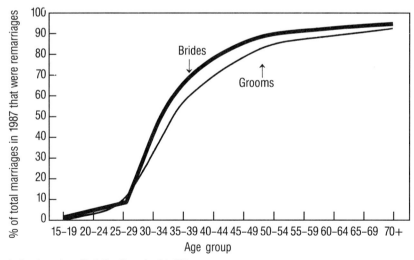

Author based on Statistics Canada, 84–205
Note: Legal marriages only.

STAR PHOENIX
Jan. 4/90

VANCOUVER SUN 29/09/88

Too many Toronto homes by 2000?

Aging population expected to alter housing demands

TORONTO STAR 11/4/9

AGED
NO
FUN
FOR
MDs

London Free Press 2/5/89

Facing the single-parent challenge

OTTAWA BUSINESS NEWS   MARCH 11-24, 1989

THE GREYING OF CANADA

TORONTO STAR 17/2/89

Number of Canadians 65 and over increasing quickly, new figures show

OTTAWA BUSINESS NEWS 8-21/4/89

Aging Population Opens New Business Opportunities

THE VANCOUVER SUN 1/10/88

Starter home will be thing of the past, expert predicts

GLOBE & MAIL 27/5/89

Growing old in Canada

OTTAWA CITIZEN 30/10/88

Aging of population to have profound implications

Financial Post 15/5/89

Many marketers missing bets by ignoring over-50s

Household Trends Into the Future:

Husband-Wife Families Are the Shrinking Majority

We all live in households, and households are changing quickly.

The makeup of households is shifting rapidly to more non-family units. The never married, the divorced, and single-parent families are surging ahead in numbers. Married husband-wife families are the slowest growing type of household in Canada.

Under a "continued change" social scenario, the number of households will increase rapidly over the next 10 to 15 years. This growth in the number of Canadian households will be followed by a period of no growth and then by a period of decline. This decline suggests a sharp drop in housing starts and possibly house prices at that time.

The future will see households made up of unattached individuals continuing to constitute a growing share of the total. By the year 2036 one-quarter of all households will be headed by the single, widowed, and divorced.

The greywave will be so strong that by the year 2036 over one-third of all households will be headed by a person 65 years of age or over. The "swinging singles" will be the elderly.

People Pattern No. 21
Singles Lead Household Growth

Canadian households are changing rapidly and in the process are transforming traditional views held by society. The last decade has been marked by accelerated change.

The number of private Canadian households increased by 1.8 million between 1976 and 1986 to reach almost 9 million. This represents an advance of about 25 percent in a period of only 10 years.

Family households (a group of individuals sharing a common dwelling who are related by blood, marriage, or adoption) and non-family households (persons living alone or with a group of unrelated individuals) have each contributed about half of the total increase.

The approximately equal contribution has been realized even though family households constituted 78 percent of all households at the beginning of the period. In percentage terms, family households grew by 17 percent from 1976 to 1986; non-family households increased by a huge 57 percent during the same time period.

Husband-wife families have experienced the smallest advance of any of the household types with an increase of only 14 percent. Within this group, the number of common-law couples increased much faster than the legally married.

The fastest increase of household type between 1976 to 1986 has been in households comprised of widowed and divorced individuals, followed closely by a big jump in single never-married households. Both advanced by more than 55 percent.

Single-parent households headed by men increased by almost 55 percent, with female single-parent families increasing by 46 percent.

By age group, the fastest growing households were those with heads aged 25–44 and 65 and over.

And so what . . . The strength of the trend to non-family households has always taken forecasters by surprise. The booming divorce rate, fewer children, and workaholic trends suggest that the singles' scene (never marrieds and divorced) will grow even faster.

Households by Selected Characteristics

Husband-wife families had the slowest rate of increase among household types.

	1976	1986	Change 1976–1986	
	(Thousands)	(Thousands)	(Thousands)	(%)
TOTAL Private Households	7,166	8,992	1,826	+25.5
By Type				
Family Households	5,605	6,543	938	+16.7
Non-Family Households	1,561	2,449	888	+56.8
By Marital Status				
Husband-Wife (Includes common-law)				
With or without children	5,088	5,782	694	+13.6
Single Parents				
—Female Head	430	627	197	+45.8
—Male Head	86	134	47	+54.6
Singles				
No Children				
—Widowed, Divorced	821	1,299	479	+58.3
—Never Married	740	1,149	409	+55.3
By Age Group				
15–24	582	515	−67	−11.6
25–44	3,020	4,091	1,071	+35.4
45–64	2,384	2,755	371	+15.6
65+	1,180	1,631	451	+38.2

Author based on Statistics Canada, 1976 and 1986 Census

People Pattern No. 22

Household Creation, "Continued Change" or "Frozen Status" Social Scenarios

The household is the basic Canadian building block. It is the key unit of society, whether it is comprised of single individuals or families.

Forecasts of household numbers depend on population projections and assumptions about the types of households individuals will form as they pass through life. Will the proportion of single never-married persons continue to rise? Will the divorce rate climb? Will single parents raise their own children? Will remarriages increase? There are many hard questions, but no easy answers.

Statistics Canada has developed a household forecasting model that implicitly addresses the broad range of questions noted above. The results outlined here are based on two social scenarios developed by Statistics Canada and applied to the "most likely" population forecast discussed in People Patterns 5 and 6. The first social scenario can be best labelled "continued change," in which the trend lines experienced during the last decade are assumed to continue into the next century. The second scenario can be referred to as "frozen status" because all the social patterns are assumed to remain frozen at their 1986 levels. I believe the "continued change" scenario is much more likely to occur.

The "continued change" social scenario results in a larger number of households because of the assumption that there are more singles and single parents. According to this scenario, the number of households will increase by over 2 million during the 1986 to 1996 period, by almost 1.8 million during the 1996 to 2006 period, and then will begin to slow quickly. The number of households will peak near 14.5 million around the year 2031 and then decline.

The "frozen status" social scenario produces fewer but bigger households, with the peak at 13.5 million – a whole 1 million fewer households than under the "continued change" social scenario. The number of households will also peak in 2031 and then decline.

And so what ... The building industry will have to track the evolution of social change to ensure that the type and amount of housing demanded is in fact supplied. The projected slowdown in about 20 years and then decline in actual household numbers in about 40 years points to a sharp drop in housing starts and possibly house prices at that time.

Total Household Projections

A peak in household numbers will occur in about 40 years under both assumptions concerning social change.

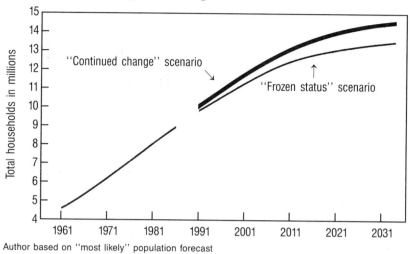

Author based on "most likely" population forecast

Projected Change in Number of Households

Household numbers will increase more quickly if the social change evident in the past continues to evolve.

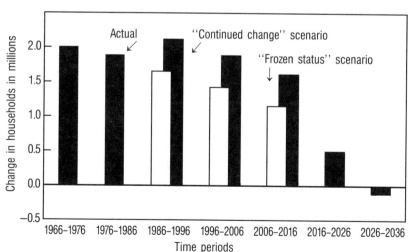

Author based on "most likely" population forecast

People Pattern No. 23
Seniors Will Be the "Swinging Singles"

The future makeup of Canadian households will be shaped by both the changing age structure and the tendency to form smaller households.

The "continued change" social scenario results in a very rapid increase in non-family households. Between now and the year 2036, the number of non-family units headed by unattached individuals is projected to increase by 2.8 million, while the number of families will increase by 2.6 million. Households of unattached individuals will rise from about 28 percent of all households currently to over 36 percent by the year 2036. The number of households comprised of unattached individuals will more than double, compared with an increase of 40 percent for families.

The most rapidly increasing segment of households of unattached individuals will be those comprised of widowed or divorced persons with no children at home; their numbers will triple between now and the year 2036. This group will then form over one-quarter of all households; they form about 15 percent now. A startling feature of the projected number of households headed by widowed and divorced unattached individuals is that two out of every three households will be headed by people 65 years of age or over. Of those 65 and over there will be two households headed by a woman for every household headed by a man.

Single never-married and lone-parent households will increase more slowly because, as seen in People Patterns 5 to 9, the actual number of young persons, who form the majority of this group, will continue to decline over the next several decades as the fertility rate falls.

Husband-wife families, including couples in a common-law relationship, will increase slowly during the entire period. Their share of all households will decline from 64 percent of all households now to 56 percent by 2036.

And so what... The number of single, widowed, and divorced people will surge to constitute over one-quarter of all households. This will revolutionize the view Canadians have of singles, with over two-thirds of the singles being senior citizens. The elderly singles will need to develop both their internal feelings of completeness and wholeness as well as build friendships with others to fill their need for intimacy and social interaction.

Predicted Types of Households

Households headed by unattached individuals will outpace the growth of families.

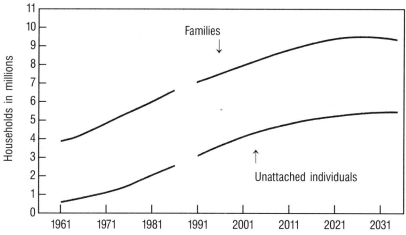

Author based on "most likely" population forecast, and "continued change" social scenario

Predicted Marital Status Within Households

Households headed by people who are childless, widowed, or divorced will experience the fastest growth in the future.

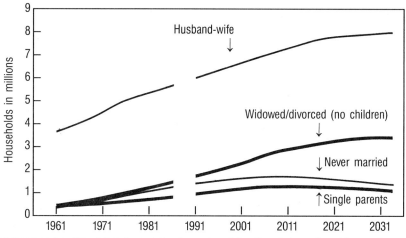

Author based on "most likely" population forecast, and "continued change" social scenario

People Pattern No. 24

A Future with More Middle-Aged and Elderly Households

The present population base and the normal process of aging will have an impact on the structure of future households. Today's young households will become the future's senior households.

The number of households headed by young adults aged 15–24 peaked in the early 1980s as the last of the baby boomers left home. The number of households headed by people 15 to 24 years old declined sharply during the 1980s, and there will now be a more gradual reduction over the next several decades. The low fertility rate will keep this group small.

The aging of the baby boomers has already had an expansionary impact on the number of households headed by 25–44 year olds. The size of this group has been increasing by about 1 million during each of the last two decades. The mid-1990s will see the 25–44 age group peak near 5 million households and then decline.

The fastest growing group of households now and over the next two complete decades will be those headed by people aged 45–64. Between 1991 and 2001 the number of households headed by this group will jump by 1 million and will do so again between 2001 and 2011. The peak for the group will be at 5.3 million around 2016, or some 20 years after the peak for the 25–44 group and some 35 years after the peak for the 15–24 age group. The forecast of households by age structure follows the normal aging pattern and thus is quite reliable for several decades into the future.

Households headed by persons aged 65 and over have grown and will continue to grow in number. The smooth and steady growth is remarkable and will result in the 65 and over age group heading over 36 percent of all households by 2036, compared with about 18 percent now. In 2036, every third household will be headed by a senior citizen.

By 2036, 70 percent of all households will be headed by people 45 years of age and over; less than 50 percent of households now are headed by people in that age group.

And so what . . . Over the next two decades the needs of households that are centred on the middle-aged will predominate but in time will be supplemented by the needs of households centred on the elderly. One-story housing and elevators will become more popular.

Households by Age of Head

The number of household heads aged 45 and over will boom over the next several decades.

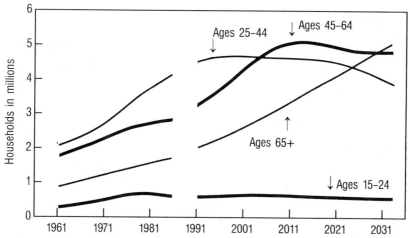

Author based on "most likely" population forecast, and "continued change" social scenario.

Detailed Household Projections by Age of Head

Elderly households will more than triple in number over the next half century.

Year	Total Households	Number of Households (Thousands)				% of Total Households			
		Ages 15-24	Ages 25-44	Ages 45-64	Ages 65+	Ages 15-24	Ages 25-44	Ages 45-64	Ages 65+
1986	8,991	514	4,091	2,755	1,631	5.7	45.5	30.6	18.1
1991	9,994	457	4,572	3,029	1,936	4.6	45.7	30.3	19.4
1996	10,996	449	4,793	3,509	2,245	4.1	43.5	31.9	20.4
2001	11,950	465	4,889	4,084	2,512	3.9	40.9	34.2	21.0
2006	12,789	476	4,825	4,726	2,762	3.7	37.7	36.9	21.6
2011	13,526	462	4,749	5,203	3,112	3.4	35.1	38.5	23.0
2016	14,022	420	4,725	5,277	3,600	3.0	33.6	37.6	25.7
2021	14,348	385	4,662	5,189	4,112	2.7	32.5	36.2	28.7
2026	14,507	362	4,490	5,017	4,638	2.5	30.9	34.6	31.9
2031	14,512	348	4,229	4,873	5,062	2.4	29.1	33.6	34.9
2036	14,378	336	3,925	4,864	5,253	2.3	27.3	33.8	36.5

Author based on "most likely" population forecast, and "continued change" social scenario.

More Canadians are choosing self-employment

FEDERAL BUSINESS DEVELOPMENT BANK

SPRING 1989

Business Ownership

An Attractive Option for Canadian Youth

Job creation hides labor market problems

Girls need computers, 'not dolls'

Attitude to women working has changed over the years

Women in professional occupation

Are small businesses nation's big employers?

ENTREPRENEURSHIP FLOURISHING

Youth take risks

Changing Labour Markets:

Women, Women, and Even More Women

The recession-depression of the early 1980s has been a key force in transforming the way people look at work due in large part to the fact that the number of unemployed has remained above 1 million since the downturn.

The movement of women into the paid labour force continues unabated, with 7 out of every 10 new jobs created in the last decade going to women. Women increased their share of the full-time job market while maintaining a steady share of all part-time jobs.

Part-time jobs increased throughout the recession-depression of the early 1980s while the number of full-time jobs suffered wide variations.

The number of self-employed people increased at more than twice the pace of those working for others. The most rapid growth in self-employment was in the finance, insurance, and real estate industries.

Uncertainty, restlessness, and strained budgets have caused a doubling in the numbers of employed people looking for other work, with the biggest increase among men 45 years of age and older.

The number of people moonlighting increased sharply, especially for women, such that women are now just as likely as men to hold down a second job.

People Pattern No. 25
The Ups and Downs of Working

The number of Canadians currently holding down jobs is at an all-time high. Even so, unemployment remains at socially unacceptable levels as the impact of the recession-depression during the early 1980s remains with us.

Over the last two decades, the economy was on average able to create about 225,000 jobs each year. The best-ever years were 1973 and 1979, when over 400,000 new jobs were added. More recently, the 383,000 jobs created in 1988 ranked as third highest in over two decades. In 1989, the number of job holders advanced by about 250,000.

The year 1982 was the worst of the post-war period in terms of employment. The number of working Canadians plummetted by almost 400,000 people. This was followed by a weak 1983 when only 57,000 new jobs were created. The downturn in 1982 was so severe that the previous 1981 peak in the number of total job holders was not reached again until the year 1985. The 1982 downturn was by far the worst since the depression of the 1930s, and its impact is still with us. The downturn has been labelled a recession-depression due to its severity.

The number of unemployed people "who are actively looking for work but are unsuccessful" rose gradually throughout the late 1960s and the 1970s before soaring during the early 1980s. The number of Canadians who were unemployed during 1983 and 1984 averaged about 1,400,000 compared with less than 900,000 just prior to the recession-depression. During 1982, over 3 million Canadians experienced some bouts of unemployment. Unemployment still remains above the 1 million mark. It is noteworthy that unemployment had never risen above half a million before the 1970s.

Canada's unemployment rate has risen from about 4 percent during the late 1960s, to a range of 5 to 8 percent during the 1970s, and to almost 12 percent in 1983. Since then, the unemployment rate declined for six consecutive years and has recently fluctuated around 7 to 8 percent. It is rising again as the 1990s begin. People Patterns 38 to 41 look at unemployment in more detail.

And so what... The volatile movements in the labour market, especially the 1982 downturn, have caused the typical worker to become less certain about the future. This uncertainty has lead to modest wage increases (less than inflation) and more people entering the labour market in order to sustain household incomes. The result may be the rise of the workaholic family discussed in People Pattern 32.

Labour Force Trends

A general upward trend for labour force and employment was temporarily interrupted by the serious recession of the early 1980s.

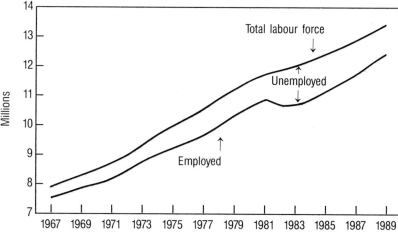

Author based on Statistics Canada, 71–529

Unemployment Rate

Canada's unemployment rate has recovered from its disastrous rise during the early 1980s.

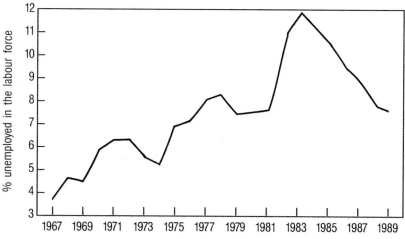

Author based on Statistics Canada, 71-529

People Pattern No. 26
Women Get Most New Jobs

A revolution is occurring in the job market with women holding down a bigger share of all the jobs. The best gains have been in full-time jobs.

Between 1979 and 1989, the number of people working in Canada increased by just under 2.1 million. Of this total increase, just under 1.5 million of these workers were women. In more precise terms, 71 percent, or over 7 out of every 10 new jobs created in Canada, went to women during the decade. By 1989, women held 44 percent of all the jobs; they held 39 percent a decade earlier and less than one-third of the total only two decades before.

Some people claim that most of the jobs going to women are part-time. This statement is true only to the extent that part-time jobs held by both men and women have increased more than full-time jobs over the last decade. Women have maintained their 72 percent share of all part-time jobs while increasing their share of the full-time jobs. Of the full-time jobs created, a growing share are held by women, up by 5 percentage points over the last decade.

The female/male employment income differential has narrowed over the medium-term but has not improved since the mid-1980s (see People Pattern 45).

On average, women have been in their current jobs for shorter periods than men. Women have been employed at the same job for an average of only 5.8 years compared with 8.4 years for men. This differential also seems to be narrowing. Since the recession of 1982, the average duration of a job held by women has increased by over five months, while the average duration of jobs held by men fell by over three months.

And so what . . . The rapid entry of women into the labour market is proceeding with little negative "backlash" from male workers. Tough issues still need to be resolved: will women be able to move into the top jobs, which have traditionally been the preserve of men? Will the income disadvantage narrow further? Will men play a bigger role in carrying out household tasks?

Employment Levels

Women got 7 out of every 10 new jobs in Canada during the last decade.

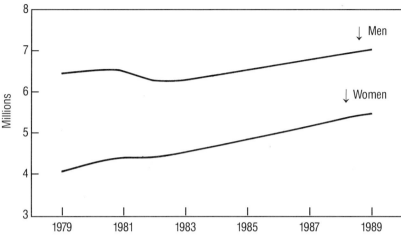

Author based on Statistics Canada, 71–529

Women's Share of Total Jobs

Women have made steady gains in the full-time job market and also held their share of part-time jobs.

Year	Total (%)	Full-time (%)	Part-time (%)
1979	38.8	34.0	72.1
1983	41.9	36.6	71.3
1989	44.1	39.2	71.6

Author based on Statistics Canada, 71–529

People Pattern No. 27
Part-Time Jobs and the Recession

The number of part-time jobs (less than 30 hours per week) increased by over 45 percent during the last decade, or by almost three times the pace of growth in full-time jobs.

The shift to part-time jobs was especially strong during the recession-depression of 1982 as the growth in full-time jobs disappeared. From a peak in 1981, the number of full-time jobs fell by almost 500,000 during the recession and did not return to the previous peak until five years later. In contrast, the number of part-time jobs continued to grow each and every year during the entire decade. This steady year-to-year increase in part-time employment was evident for both men and women. By 1989, part-time jobs represented over 15 percent of all jobs in Canada.

Not only are part-time jobs growing in importance but they are being worked at more hours per week. In 1989, the average part-time job provided 16.3 hours of work per week. A decade earlier, it provided 15.2 hours per week. The more than 1-hour increase for part-time jobs is larger than the 0.9-hour increase for full-time jobs. Longer work weeks have returned. See the comments on the new "workaholic family" in People Pattern 32.

The relative abundance of part-time jobs as compared with full-time jobs is one reason why people are working part-time. In 1983, 30 percent of both men and women who worked part time said they did so because they could only find part-time jobs. Even now, this "could only find part-time jobs" response still remains much higher than before the recession for both sexes.

In more general terms, the main reason why men work part-time is because they are going to school. Traditionally, the main reason given by women for having part-time jobs was because they did not want full-time jobs. Part-time jobs still allowed them to fulfill family responsibilities. The reasons given by women for having part-time jobs have changed significantly over the last decade, with more women working part-time simply because they "could only find part-time" jobs.

And so what ... The growing role of part-time jobs reflects the increased flexibility concerning reduced overtime hours, fewer benefits, and easier layoffs sought by many employers. The aging and reduced mobility of the labour force will make finding part-time workers more difficult and will require an upgrading of benefits and protection offered to part-time employees.

Number of Part-Time Employees

Part-time jobs have grown faster than full-time jobs for both men and women.

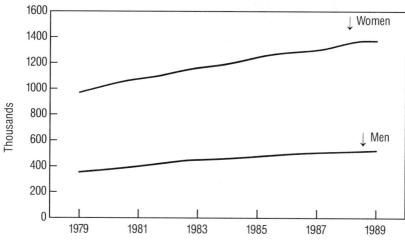

Author based on Statistics Canada, 71–529

Reasons for Part-Time Employment

Fewer women are now working part-time for strictly personal reasons or because of family responsibilities.

Year	Personal or Family Responsibility (%)	Going To School (%)	Could Only Find Part-Time (%)	Did Not Want Full-Time (%)
Men				
1979	0.0	56.7	17.4	16.8
1983	0.0	45.1	30.6	15.5
1989	0.9	55.2	22.0	18.3
Women				
1979	15.7	20.6	17.0	43.3
1983	12.8	17.6	27.6	39.2
1989	13.6	23.2	22.3	39.3

Author based on Statistics Canada, 71–529

People Patterns No. 28
The Self-Employed are for Real

There is a rapid growth in the number of people who are setting up their own businesses. Over 13 of every 100 working people are now out on their own. This group comprises almost 1.7 million people.

Since 1981, 22 out of every 100 jobs created in Canada have been in self-employment. Over the 1981 to 1989 period, self-employment increased by 24 percent, which is more than double the increase in the number of individuals who work for others. In spite of this expansion, roughly 87 percent of all Canadian workers are still "employees." Many of these employees work for the self-employed.

The most rapid growth has been for self-employed women. From 1981 to 1989, the numbers of self-employed women increased by 52 percent; the numbers of self-employed men increased by only 15 percent. Even so, self-employed men still constitute 71 percent of all of the self-employed in Canada. In 1981, 76 percent of all the self-employed were men.

During the 1980s, the finance, insurance, and real estate sectors experienced the most rapid growth in self-employment (about 63 percent). Next in line was growth in self-employment in services and construction. Agriculture was the only sector where the number of self-employed declined.

Over two-thirds of the self-employed are operating businesses that are unincorporated. The self-employed who are most likely to be incorporated are in manufacturing and construction. The smallest level of incorporation is in agriculture.

And so what . . . Self-employment represents an opportunity for the entrepreneurial to do their own thing, and it offers an escape from unemployment for those who want to but cannot find suitable employee-type jobs. The growing number of double-income households and older workers will make self-employment easier to achieve.

Number of Self-Employed Workers

The rapid growth of the self-employed and entrepreneurs has been a notable feature of the 1980s.

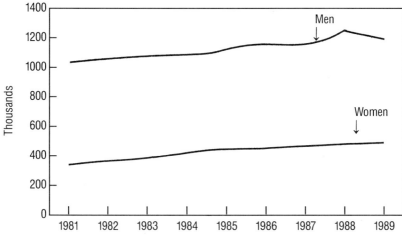

Author based on Statistics Canada, 71–529

Self-Employed by Industry

The fastest growing area for the self-employed has been the financial, insurance, and real estate sector.

Industry	1981 (Thousands)	1989 (Thousands)	% Change 1981–1989
Finance, Insurance, and Real Estate	40	65	62.5
Services	418	597	42.8
Construction	161	220	36.6
Manufacturing	72	87	20.8
Transportation, Communication, Utilities	58	71	22.4
Other Primary	36	43	19.4
Trade	300	341	13.7
Agriculture	268	250	−6.7
TOTAL	1,353	1,674	23.7

Author based on Statistics Canada, 71–529

People Pattern No. 29
More Looking Around and Moonlighting

The number of employees who are looking around for "greener pastures" and those who are moonlighting are both increasing rapidly.

In 1981, about 2 percent of all people who already had a full-time job were looking for work elsewhere. By 1989, the number of full-time workers who were looking for other work had more than doubled to 4.3 percent. The percentage of part-time workers who were looking also doubled to almost 10 percent.

Among full-time workers, the "looking around" has affected the 15–24 and 25–44 age groups in a similar fashion, with a doubling for both groups. A tripling occurred for the 45 and over age group.

The percentage of those under 25 who have a full-time job but are looking for another rose from about 4 percent in 1981 to over 8 percent in 1989. Among the 25–44 group, those searching rose from under 2 percent to over 4 percent. The biggest change in the number of full-time employees looking for another job was evident for the 45 and over category, with a tripling for both men and women. By 1989, about 1.5 percent of this group were looking elsewhere. Looking around clearly declines with age.

For all part-time workers, the number looking for another job also doubled from 5 percent to almost 10 percent. About 15 percent of male part-time workers aged 25–44 were looking for another job in 1981. This rose to as high as 33 percent during the mid-1980s and is still above 25 percent.

Moonlighting was reported by 3.4 percent of all workers in 1981. By 1989, 4.6 percent of all workers were moonlighting. The biggest jump in multiple job holders was among women, such that by 1989, 4.6 percent of women also held down more than one job. In contrast to 1981, when less than 3 percent of women were moonlighting, women are now just as likely to have second jobs as are men. The total number of moonlighters was 575,000 in 1989.

And so what... Increased looking around and moonlighting suggests that more people have strained budgets, that they are not being challenged by their present jobs, or that they are feeling less secure about the longevity of the jobs they now hold. Workers seem to be getting more restless than they were a decade ago.

People Aged 25–44 with Job but Looking

More and more workers with jobs are looking for work elsewhere.

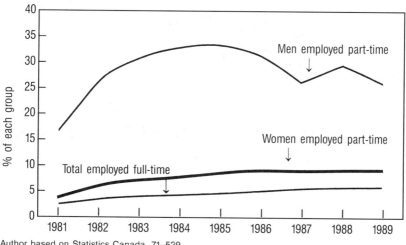

Author based on Statistics Canada, 71–529

Rate of Employee Moonlighting

Women are now just as likely to have a second job as are men.

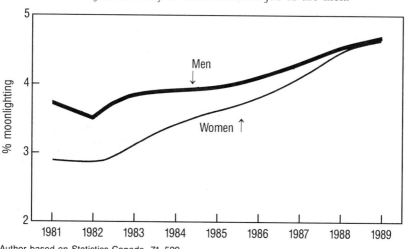

Author based on Statistics Canada, 71–529

THE TORONTO STAR, NOV. 24/89

The day-care dilemma

GLOBE & MAIL Dec. 14/89

Moonlighting on rise
Statscan study says

OTTAWA CITIZEN 21/3/89

Both spouses in labor force
in 54% of two-parent families

Newfoundland and Labrador's Business Newspaper, May 1989

Record number of mothers working
outside the home

The Globe and Mail 26/05/89

Maternity leave most attractive
to Canada's early 30s, study says

TORONTO STAR 16/3/89

More than half
of Canadians
work all year

OTTAWA CITIZEN
13/4/89

Working women
grow by 21%

GLOBE & MAIL 14/4/89

Declining fertility rate
is verdict on economy

The Financial Post 08/05/1989

Day care costs plenty, but companies
provide it to promote efficiency and
employee goodwill

MONTREAL GAZETTE
13/4/89

More moms
taking jobs

The Leader-Post Regina, Saskatchewan Wednesday, October 17, 1984

Multiple job holders work long hours

New Canadian Workaholics:

Dad Works, Mom Works, Kid Works, and Relatives Work

The greater involvement of women and other family members in the labour force has more than offset the slow decline in participation of mature men. The "workaholics" now seem to include most of the family.

The decade began with women who stayed home being in the majority. By the end of the decade women who worked "outside the home" were in a clear and substantial majority. In contrast, the labour force participation of all men 25 years of age or over declined.

The new reality includes the fact that the majority of women with children are in the paid labour market. In all cases, women with children are now more likely to be working outside the home if the husband also has a job. This new trend suggests that affordability of day-care may be a key factor in enabling women to enter the labour market.

The "workaholic family" was born in the 1980s with over two-thirds of husband-wife families now having two earners, a growing majority of single children who are still living at home in the job market, and a majority of other relatives who are living in the same household also working.

Both part-time and full-time workers are now working longer hours than at the beginning of the decade.

People Pattern No. 30
Fewer Men and More Women Want to Work

A study of contrasts! A slowly declining proportion of men of working age are in the labour force, while a sharply increasing proportion of women are working outside the home.

In 1979, 78.5 percent of all men aged 15 and over were in the labour market, being either employed or looking for work. By 1989, the male participation rate had fallen to 76.7 percent. In contrast, the rate of labour force participation for women jumped from 49 percent in 1979 to 57.9 percent in 1989, a large advance of 8.9 percentage points. Women who do not work outside the home are now the minority.

The decline in male participation rates during the decade was evident for all age groups except for 15–24 year olds. The biggest decline of over 10 percentage points was for men aged 55–64 years, where the rate fell from 76.4 percent in 1979 to 66.1 percent in 1989. This major decline reflects the much longer duration of unemployment for mature males, as outlined in People Pattern 39, and the declining rate of poverty among seniors.

The dramatic jump in female participation in jobs outside the home occurred for all age groups except for women 65–69 years of age. The largest advances were for each of the three age groups, 25–34, 35–44, and 45–54, where the increases were all above 15 percentage points.

By 1989, three-quarters of all women 25–44 years of age were in the out-of-home labour market. Over two-thirds of all women aged 15–24 and 45–54 were in the job market.

Forecasts of participation rates point to continued declines for men and increases for women. By the year 2001, the differences between the sexes will have narrowed significantly and by the year 2036 they may be negligible.

And so what . . . The massive movement of women into the work force is a key trend, one which will mark the 1990s and beyond. The ability of companies to offer true equality to both sexes will be a major challenge. More working women will mean fewer babies and a critical need for quality day-care.

Participation in the Labour Force

The decade was marked by rising participation of women in the job market at the same time as men were dropping out.

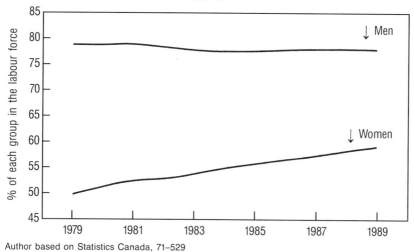

Author based on Statistics Canada, 71–529

Participation in the Labour Force by Age and Sex

Women aged 25–54 have made the largest gains in labour force participation.

	1979 (%)	1989 (%)	Change 1979–1989 (%)
Men			
15–24	71.3	73.0	+1.7
25–34	95.7	94.2	−1.6
35–44	96.3	94.8	−1.5
45–54	92.7	91.8	−0.9
55–64	76.4	66.1	−10.3
65–69	24.4	16.9	−7.5
70+	9.1	7.1	−2.0
TOTAL	78.5	76.7	−1.8
Women			
15–24	61.0	67.4	+6.4
25–34	60.4	76.2	+15.8
35–44	59.4	77.2	+17.8
45–54	52.1	67.6	+15.5
55–64	34.0	34.4	+0.4
65–69	8.2	7.5	−0.7
70+	1.9	2.1	+0.2
TOTAL	49.0	57.9	+8.9

Author based on Statistics Canada, 71–529

Mother Works if Husband Works

The presence of children affects the participation of women in the labour market. New data covering the 1980s reveal startling labour market trends that suggest that whether or not a married woman works depends significantly on the employment status of her husband.

Women with pre-school children are entering the labour force in record numbers. In addition, in 1989, almost two-thirds of all women with children under 16 years of age were in the labour force, up from 55 percent in 1981.

The chart at the top of the opposite page reveals that the biggest increase in participation rates for women with pre-school children was for women who have a husband who is employed. The participation rates for these women advanced from 48 percent to 65 percent over the 1981 to 1989 period. Women with husbands who are unemployed or not in the labour force also experienced a rapid jump in participation rates, from 41 percent in 1981 to 53 percent in 1989. In contrast, participation rates of mothers with no husbands fluctuated around 51 percent throughout the decade. The latter group had the highest participation rate in 1981 but the lowest in 1989.

Women with no pre-schoolers but with children aged 6 to 15 have also experienced rising participation in the labour market, as evident in the bottom chart. By 1989, the participation of women with working husbands was at its highest level ever (up to 77 percent). Next in line was participation by women with no husbands (up to 74 percent). An advance occurred for women with unemployed husbands who were not in the labour force (up to 58 percent).

Women under 55 years of age with no children under the age of 16 continue to be more likely to work than women with younger children.

And so what . . . The reality that the presence of employed husbands leads to higher labour force participation rates by mothers with young children suggests that affordability of day-care is a key consideration for women deciding to work outside of the home. More subsidized day-care would likely encourage more women with children but without husbands to enter the labour force. The upcoming labour shortage will make this more likely.

Women in the Labour Force with Pre-Schoolers

By 1989, two-thirds of women with pre-school children and a working husband were in the labour force.

Author based on Satistics Canada, 71–529

Women in the Labour Force with
Children Ages 6 to 15 and No Pre-Schoolers

Mothers with children ages 6 to 15 increased their participation in the labour force whatever their marital status.

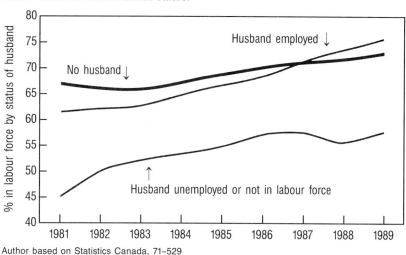

Author based on Statistics Canada, 71–529

People Pattern No. 32
The Canadian Workaholic Family

The typical Canadian family is increasingly becoming a "workaholic" unit. There are more double-income families, a growing percentage of single youth still living at home are in the labour force, and other relatives living in the same household are now participating in the labour market.

In 1979, there were approximately 2.7 million husband-wife families (including common-law relationships) with both spouses in the job market. By 1989, the number of double-income households had risen to over 3.7 million. The percentage change in double-income families is twice the growth in the total labour force.

In 1979, about 55 percent of husband-wife families under 65 years of age had both partners earning some employment or self-employment income during the year. By 1987, the ratio had risen to 66 percent and is now climbing to over 70 percent. To put it differently, there are "only" one out of three husband-wife families in which both partners do not work outside of the home. The percentage of double-income families would be much lower if couples aged over 65 were included in the calculation.

More single children who are still living at home (15 years of age and over) are also working outside the home. In 1989, about 69 percent were in the labour market, up from 60 percent a decade earlier. In part, the declining number of young people is pulling the remaining youth into the labour force. People Pattern 40 reveals that youth unemployment rates are now relatively lower than during the early part of the decade.

Other relatives living with the family (such as parents, sisters, and brothers of the head of the household) also increased their participation in the job market from 46 percent in 1979 to 53 percent in 1989.

The actual number of hours worked at both full-time and part-time jobs increased during the decade.

The trend is clear: the Canadian family is increasingly becoming orientated to working opportunities outside the home.

And so what . . . The traditional family was centred around a working father who supported a wife and children. This traditional family now represents less than one-third of all husband-wife families. The family is now made up of busy people who increasingly view the home as a place to rest and relax between work periods. Family meals are becoming less frequent and more rushed, and family activities now usually occur with one or more family members absent.

Family in the Labour Force

Higher labour force participation by husbands and wives, by single children, and by relatives living with families points to the emergence of a new "workaholic family."

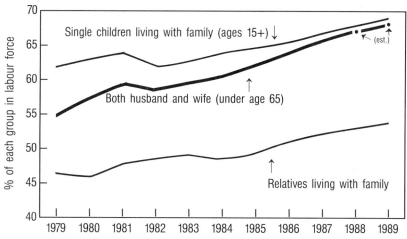

Author based on Satistics Canada, 71–529, and unpublished data

Actual Hours Worked per Week

Both full-timers and part-timers were working longer hours in 1989 compared with 1979.

	1979	1989
Full-Time Jobs	41.5	42.4
Part-Time Jobs	15.2	16.3

Author based on Statistics Canada, 71–529
Note: Average hours, excluding people not at work

Work force quantity, quality seen as key in year 2000

The Toronto Star 23/06/89

GLOBE & MAIL 23/1/89

Shortage of skills to worsen in '90s

Canada to remain favored target for immigrants, study predicts

A10 THE GLOBE AND MAIL, THURSDAY, JANUARY 4, 1990

OTTAWA CITIZEN 10/2/89

Skilled workers scarce: survey

The Ottawa Citizen 15/6/89

Investment firms tap into women's growing pool of capital

TORONTO STAR 6/3/89

Immigrants: Take in more or face crisis Canada told

GLOBE & MAIL Oct. 10/88

Labor crisis in 1990s predicted

Supreme Court will decide fate of mandatory retirement issue

LONDON FREE PRESS 2/5/89

The family roles are shifting

Labour Force Trends into the Future:

"Severe" Shortages Will Boost Wages and Immigration

The twenty-first century will see the emergence of a severe labour shortage in Canada. The labour force will likely begin to shrink in 20 to 25 years. The labour shortage will come much sooner.

The shortage will occur even if the rate of women's participation in the labour force equals the rate of men's participation.

The labour shortage means that Canada will need many more immigrants to support the growth of the economy. Later retirement and the expanded use of robotics are also likely.

Young workers will increasingly be in short supply, with both declining numbers and a smaller share of the total labour force. Only a very sharp and immediate upturn in fertility could alleviate the shortage of young workers in the future, but this will not happen.

Older workers will constitute over 40 percent of the labour force in 2036; they now constitute one-quarter of the labour force.

Managerial/administrative skills will be the most in demand to the end of the century, with educational requirements rising further. Workers will need to keep up and can expect to change jobs and careers more frequently than ever before.

People Pattern No. 33
Many More Managers and Professionals

The world is changing quickly with shifts in the demands both for goods and services and for the human and technological inputs to supply them. The occupational structure points to even higher managerial and professional skill requirements in the future.

The number of people employed in managerial and administrative professional occupations more than doubled during the last decade, with the addition of almost 800,000 new jobs in this sector alone. This occupational grouping experienced the fastest growth in percentage terms: the 97 percent growth was significantly above all the other major groupings. Employment and Immigration Canada forecasts that almost 900,000 new managerial and administrative professional jobs will be created from 1986 to the end of the century.

The makeup of managerial and administrative professionals also reflects the growing importance of women in the work force. The number of female managers and administrative professionals increased over three times faster (+194 percent) in percentage terms than was the case for males (+63 percent). About 38 percent of managerial and administrative professionals are now women, up from 26 percent a decade earlier.

Service (+24 percent) and clerical (+18 percent) occupations have not grown rapidly in percentage terms during the 1979 to 1989 period, even if both of these occupations have seen total job numbers advance by about 350,000. Service jobs are expected to continue to grow at a similar pace, while clerical jobs will increase more slowly.

The educational requirements of new jobs is projected to increase further. According to Employment and Immigration Canada, the percentage of new jobs to the year 2000 that will require 17 or more years of education (post-university) will rise to almost 50 percent; currently, only 22 percent of all jobs require 17 or more years of education. One-third of the new jobs created until the end of the century will be filled by people with less than a grade 12 education, compared with 45 percent for the jobs that now exist.

And so what . . . The changing occupational structure of the work force means that both individuals and employers will need to continually assess their present skills and future requirements. Individuals can expect to, voluntarily or forcibly, change occupations several times during their working lives.

Labour Force by Occupation

Professional jobs have shown the most rapid growth in percentage terms during the decade.

	Increase in Number of Jobs Between 1979 to 1989		Share of Jobs Held by Women	
	Change (%)	Change (Thousands)	1979 (%)	1989 (%)
Managerial and Administrative Professionals	97	789	26	38
Artistic, Literary, Recreational Professionals	64	99	35	45
Social Science Professionals	47	74	51	57
Medicine and Health Professionals	36	169	77	79
Natural Sciences, Engineering and Mathematics Professionals	25	95	12	19
Services	24	352	55	57
Teaching Professionals	20	93	57	62
Clerical	18	342	77	80
Material Handling	7	21	20	21

Author based on Statistics Canada, 71–529

Job Educational Requirements

New jobs created to the year 2000 will increasingly require education beyond a basic university degree.

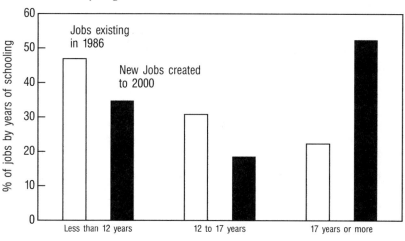

Author based on Employment and Immigration Canada, 1989

People Pattern No. 34

Higher Participation Won't Halt Decline in Labour Force

The labour force provides both the basis to create goods and services in the economy and the income to support individuals and families. The basis for growth will weaken as the total labour force will likely decline in about 25 years.

Forecasts of the number of people in the labour force are relatively easy to prepare on a computational basis. Simply multiply the forecasts of participation rates by age and sex by a forecast of the total population by age and sex. The population estimate used here is the "most likely" forecast discussed in People Pattern 5.

My labour force participation rate projections are shown on the next page. Statistical techniques, examination of other forecasts, and my view of the future were used to forecast reasonable male and female participation rates to the year 2001. After the year 2001, the male rates are assumed to remain constant to the year 2036.

The participation rate outlook for women beyond 2001 is more difficult to assess. Will the dramatic pace of change continue beyond 2001? Two different female labour force participation assumptions are made. The "rising female after 2001" scenario projects that by the year 2036 women's participation rates will be the same as for men in 2036 (which are assumed to remain at the level attained in 2001). The "stable female after 2001" scenario assumes that women's participation rates will also remain at the level they reach in 2001.

The result of this process is one labour force forecast to 2001 and two forecasts for the period 2001 to 2036. The labour force is projected to grow from 12.7 million in 1986 to over 16 million in 2001.

The "rising female after 2001" scenario sees the total labour force peaking at 17 million in 2016 and then falling back to 15.6 million by the year 2036. The "stable female after 2001" scenario projects that the labour force will peak at a lower 16.8 million around 2011 and then dip to under 15 million by the year 2036. The "stable female after 2001" scenario reduces the labour force by about 600,000 by the year 2036.

And so what . . . The Canadian labour force will likely continue to grow until the second decade of the twenty-first century. It will then decline as the baby boomers begin to retire and the projected low fertility rate reduces the number of entry-level workers still further. Much higher immigration levels will be needed to prevent the decline of the total labour force. The use of robotics will boom as employers are faced with a shortage of workers.

Projected Labour Force Participation

The degree to which each age group participates in the job market is key to labour force projections.

	% of Age Group in 2001	
Age Group	Men	Women
15–24	73.9	71.3
25–34	91.0	86.2
35–44	92.8	87.1
45–55	89.8	77.8
55–64	59.2	46.1
65–69	11.1	4.8
70+	4.9	2.0

Author

Projected Labour Force

Canada's labour force will grow more slowly and then decline as the baby boomers retire.

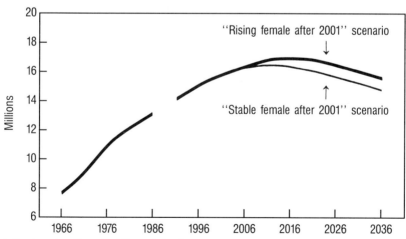

Author based on "most likely" population forecast

People Pattern No. 35
More Babies or More Immigrants?

Following a long period of rapid expansion in Canada's labour force, there will be a slowing growth and then a sharp decline. A severe labour shortage is coming (see People Patterns 5 and 9).

The total labour force increased by 1.2 million between 1966 and 1971. Labour force growth accelerated to 1.6 and 1.7 million during the 1971 to 1976 and 1976 to 1981 periods as the baby boomers entered the job market. The smaller increase of less than 1 million during the 1981 to 1986 period reflects the impact of the recession and fewer young workers.

The 1.4 million increase in the labour force projected for the 1986 to 1991 period is consistent with the average annual growth of about 250,000 experienced during each of the last few years.

The growth of the labour force is expected to slow to about 1.1 million during the 1991 to 1996 period and then slow further to less than 900,000 during the next five years to 2001. Considering both labour force participation rate scenarios (see People Pattern 34), the first decade of the twenty-first century will see a more rapid slowdown in labour force growth, with increases as low as 200,000 or as high as 600,000 during each five-year period.

The second decade of the twenty-first century (2011–2021) will usher in a completely new reality. The total labour force numbers will experience absolute declines under both participation rate scenarios. Using the "rising female after 2001" scenario, the labour force will shrink by over 300,000 during each five-year period from the year 2021. The "stable female after 2001" scenario projects that the labour force will be shrinking even faster (by up to 541,000) during each five-year period.

And so what . . . The decline in labour force numbers in about 25 years will mean fewer income earners to pay for the needs of an aging society, as discussed in People Pattern 10. Unless fertility rates begin to rise soon, the only way to sustain the labour force will be through immigration. At least 100,000 to 200,000 additional immigrants will be required each year on top of the 200,000 already considered in the "most likely" population forecast.

Projected Labour Force Change

Even if women participate in the work force to the same extent as men, the number of people available for work will still shrink, beginning in about twenty years.

Change in Labour Force (Thousands of Persons)	
1966–1971	1,146
1971–1976	1,564
1976–1981	1,696
1981–1986	959
1986–1991	1,369
1991–1996	1,078
1996–2001	871

Change in Labour Force (Thousands of Persons)		
	"Rising Female After 2001" Scenario	"Stable Female After 2001" Scenario
2001–2006	639	514
2006–2011	344	199
2011–2016	−43	−168
2016–2021	−238	−381
2021–2026	−332	−494
2026–2031	−433	−541
2031–2036	−371	−506

Author based on "most likely" population forecast

People Pattern No. 36
More Women and Older Workers in Future

The trend of having more women in the work place will continue. The work force will also get older.

The number of men in the labour force is projected to peak at near the 9 million mark during the 2011 to 2016 period. This represents an increase of over 20 percent from current levels. Following the peak, the male labour force will decline by about 1 million by the year 2036.

The number of women in the labour force will peak shortly after 2016 under the "rising female after 2001" scenario (see People Pattern 34). At the peak, over 8 million women will be in the labour force, compared with about 6 million now. The peak would come sooner and be about 300,000 lower under the "stable female after 2001" participation scenario. By 2036 the difference between the scenarios will be about 600,000 workers.

At present, women make up about 44 percent of the labour force. This share will reach 50 percent by 2036 under the "rising female after 2001" scenario or will peak near 48 percent under the "stable female after 2001" scenario.

The number of people aged 15–24 in the labour force will remain near current levels of 2.6 to 2.8 million until about 2011, when the numbers will begin to fall to 2.1 million by the year 2036. Youth's share of the total labour force will drop continually from about 20 percent now to 13 percent by 2036. In 1976, the 15–24 age group constituted roughly 27 percent of the total work force.

The number of people aged 25–44 and 45–64 in the labour force will peak in 2001 and in 2016 respectively. The share of the labour force made up by people aged 25–44 will actually decline over the forecast period. In contrast, the 45–64 age group will experience a very rapid increase from about 25 percent of the total labour force now to over 41 percent by the year 2036.

The over 65 age group will grow both in numbers and in their share of the labour force over the next 50 years.

And so what... The aging of the labour force may lead to higher productivity in the economy as both maturing and older workers reach their performance highs. The absolute decline in the size of the labour force will encourage many elderly workers to remain in the labour force beyond the normal retirement age. Even so, a severe labour shortage is likely after the year 2011. More immigration will be needed.

Labour Force Projections

Women will form a growing part of the total labour force, and under the "rising female" scenario could equal the number of men by the end of the forecast period.

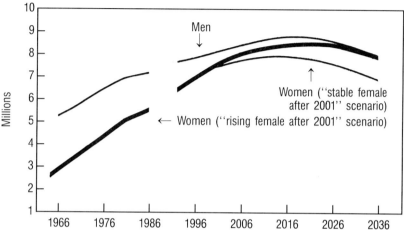

Author based on "most likely" population forecast

Detailed Labour Force Projections by Age

Young workers will constitute a shrinking share of the work force, while 45 to 64 year olds will sharply increase their share.

Year	Number of Participants (Thousands)				% of Total Labour Force			
	Ages 15–24	Ages 25–44	Ages 45–64	Ages 65+	Ages 15–24	Ages 25–44	Ages 45–64	Ages 65+
1986	2,787	6,714	3,066	178	21.9	52.7	24.1	1.4
1991	2,689	7,697	3,488	199	19.1	54.6	24.8	1.4
1996	2,706	8,040	4,252	190	17.8	52.9	28.0	1.3
2001	2,811	8,049	5,022	176	17.5	50.1	31.2	1.1
2006	2,859	7,352	5,783	206	17.1	47.0	34.6	1.2
2011	2,752	7,686	6,354	254	16.1	45.0	37.3	1.5
2016	2,512	7,705	6,465	320	14.8	45.3	38.0	1.9
2021	2,308	7,670	6,404	382	13.8	45.7	38.2	2.3
2026	2,190	7,458	6,334	449	13.3	45.4	38.5	2.7
2031	2,095	7,071	6,327	505	13.1	44.2	39.5	3.2
2036	2,031	6,638	6,422	536	12.9	42.4	41.1	3.4

Author based on "most likely" population forecast and "rising female after 2001" scenario

People Pattern No. 37
A Request to Change a Definition

This section will test your mathematical and intuitive skills. If all the parts go up or stay flat, can the total go down? The answer is yes if you are examining labour force participation rates after the year 2001.

The participation rate forecast for the years beyond 2001 presented in People Pattern 34 assumed that male rates for each of the seven age groups would remain at the rates attained in 2001 and that female rates would either reach the male rates by 2036 or would maintain the female rates attained in 2001. In all cases, the rates either remain constant or they increase.

The above might lead some people to predict that the total labour force participation rate will also remain flat or maybe even rise into the long-term future. That is incorrect!

Statistics Canada defines the participation rate for the total labour force to be the total labour force in any year divided by the total number of people aged 15 and over in the population during that year. The history and forecast for this total participation rate is shown in the top chart on the opposite page. The calculations indicate that the total participation rate will peak at about 69 percent in 2001 and then drop sharply to only 60 percent by the year 2036. This would return the total participation rate to the level reached during the mid-1970s.

The main reason for the decline in total labour force participation is the very large increase in the population of older Canadians, who have very low participation rates. In 1989, for instance, roughly 12 percent of people aged 65–69 were in the labour force, and 4 percent of those over 70 years of age were in the labour force. As these groups increase their share of the total population, the total labour participation rate will drop.

The chart at the bottom redefines the labour force to include only labour force members and population aged 15–64. Using this definition, the total participation rate still peaks in 2001 at a higher 81 percent but falls much more slowly to 79 percent by the year 2036.

And so what . . . The sharp drop forecast for total labour force participation rate using the standard measure is very misleading. The measure should be changed to include only individuals aged 15–64 years of age. This People Pattern suggests that economic and social indicators are not always as easy to interpret as they sometimes seem at first glance.

Total Labour Force Participation Rate
According to the "Standard" Definition

The standard Statistics Canada definition of labour force will lead to a misleading suggestion of reduced participation.

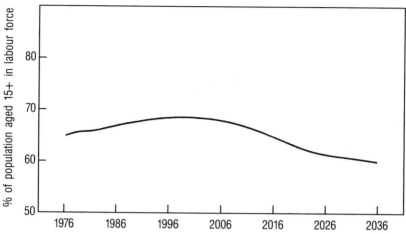

Author based on "most likely" population forecast and "rising female after 2001" scenario.

Total Labour Force Participation Rate
According to Proposed "15–64" Definition

The proposed definition shows that the participation of people in the prime working ages will be roughly maintained.

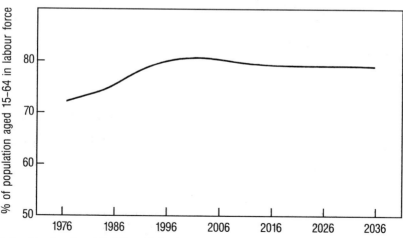

Author based on "most likely" population forecast and "rising female after 2001" scenario.

LEADER POST July 21/1984

Unemployment major issue

WINNIPEG FREE PRESS 9/10/88

Unemployment across Canada

The Leader-Post Regina, Saskatchewan Saturday, December 15, 1984

Many aren't being reported on unemployment figures

TORONTO STAR 20/4/89

When 'working for pogey' becomes way of life

The Financial Post 09/05/1989

Unemployment rates move up in both Canada and U.S.

SASKATOON, SASKATCHEWAN STAR-PHOE

10 years of poverty rob man's self-esteer

GLOBE AND MAIL DEC. 14/89

Layoffs, closings raise spectre of recession

WINNIPEG FREE PRESS 8/11/88

Falling unemployment rate good news for Tories

WEDNESDAY, JANUARY 10, 1990 SASKATOON, SASKATCHEWAN STAR-PHOENIX

Labor leaders predict militancy in '90s

SASKATOON, SASKATCHEWAN STAR-PHOENIX

Former high school teacher accepts role as househusband

The Unemployment Picture:

Who's Working and Who's Not

U nemployment is news – during the 1980s it was mostly bad news. The good news, however, was that the young were clear winners in relative terms.

The worst year for unemployment was 1983. The official rate was almost 12 percent, and about 26 percent of the labour force collected unemployment insurance at some time during the year. The official rate was back down to 7.5 percent as the decade ended.

The rise in unemployment was especially hard on men aged 45 and over. These mature workers saw the average duration of unemployment soar to over 32 weeks, with only limited improvement since then. This caused many of these men to drop out of the labour force.

The declining number of young workers has already begun to improve their relative position. At the beginning of the decade the unemployment rate for youth was almost three times higher than for prime wage earners, but by the end of the decade this was down to less than two times.

The declining use of government employment services suggests a need to revamp such services.

People Pattern No. 38
Unemployment Is More Than a News Story

The unemployment rate is the most written about economic statistic in Canada. The release of the latest monthly unemployment rate frequently ranks as the lead news story. Unemployment is more than a statistic: it reflects individual hardship for those affected.

A few words of caution are necessary when examining unemployment. The number of people reported as unemployed in a given year represents the average number of people unemployed during each of the monthly surveys conducted by Statistics Canada. The average masks the fact that the unemployed change significantly throughout the year as some people find jobs and others lose jobs. In 1989, on average just over 1 million people were unemployed each month, but during the entire year almost 3 million people collected some form of unemployment insurance.

Alternative measures of unemployment are available in addition to the official rate. The official unemployment rate stood at 7.4 percent in 1979, peaked at 11.8 percent in 1983 as a result of the recession-depression, and then declined to 7.5 percent by 1989.

The unemployment rate based on the number of people who collected unemployment insurance during the year followed a similar but not identical pattern with a peak of about 30 percent in 1982 and a decline since then.

The rate that includes discouraged unemployed individuals who have given up the job search is higher than the official rate, especially during recessionary periods.

And so what . . . Unemployment represents a first but it is to be hoped short-lived stage of hardship for those affected. The longer the unemployment period lasts, the less likely individuals will be able to regain their previous standards of living. As will be seen in People Patterns 42 to 44, the average worker saw real wages decline during the decade.

Two Unemployment Rates

While the official unemployment rate rose above 11 percent in 1982, over 30 percent of workers actually collected unemployment insurance during the year.

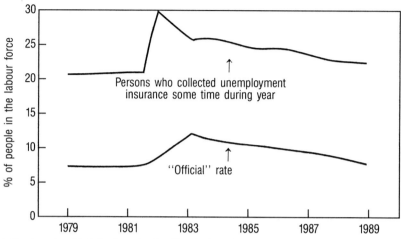

Author based on Statistics Canada, 71–429 and 73–202S

Alternative Unemployment Rates

Alternative unemployment rates provide insights into the intense debate on this issue.

	% of Persons in Labour Force		
	1979	1983	1989
"Official" Rate	7.4	11.8	7.5
Collected Unemployment Insurance during Year	20.5	25.9	21.9
"Official" plus Discouraged Workers who have Stopped Looking	8.4	13.3	8.2

Author based on Statistics Canada, 71–529 and 73–202S

People Pattern No. 39
Toughest Times for Older Workers

The recession-depression of the early 1980s has had a long-term negative impact on the duration of unemployment for older workers. Young workers have fared much better.

Before the onslaught of the recession, the average duration of unemployment for all Canadians was about 15 weeks, or approaching 4 months. The average duration soared to 22 weeks in 1983 and remained above 20 weeks until 1987. This hard data clearly reveals that during the entire period from 1983 to 1987 the average unemployed person was out of work for 5 to 5.5 months. By 1989, the average duration of unemployment fell to 17.9 weeks but still remained higher than prior to the recession.

For both men and women aged 15–24, the average duration of unemployment peaked in 1983 and then subsequently declined in 1989 to a level that was actually below the 1979 level. The average duration of unemployment for those aged 15–24 stood at just above 11 weeks in 1989. The next People Pattern concludes that youth are gaining regarding unemployment rates.

The average duration of unemployment for the 25–44 age group was about 16 weeks in 1979. The average rose sharply for men, peaking at 25 weeks in 1983 and improving to 20 weeks by 1989. For women a peak was reached in 1985 and then the rate fell. For both sexes, the average duration in 1989 was still above the average duration a decade earlier.

Those aged 45 and over have been hit the hardest as the average duration of unemployment continued to rise for both men and women until 1985 and 1986 repectively. In 1989, the average duration of unemployment among men aged 45 and over was 28 weeks. From 1985 to 1987, over 20 percent (or 1 in 5) of unemployed men aged 45 and over had been unemployed for over one full year; before the recession only 8 out of 100 had been unemployed for such a long period. Some improvement took place to 1989.

And so what... The much longer average duration of unemployment for older workers is very bad news both for workers and for the economy in general. This increased period of unemployment helps to explain why many older male workers have become discouraged and have left the job market completely as was described in People Pattern 30. An aging labour force suggests that the average duration of unemployment will tend to rise. Unemployment programs should examine the possibility of instituting longer benefit periods for mature workers compared with younger workers.

Average Weeks of Unemployment

During the 1980s, the average duration of unemployment rose for all groups except for young workers.

	1979	Peak	1989	Change in Weeks 1979-1989
TOTAL	14.8	21.8 (1983)	17.9	+3.1
Men				
15–24	12.5	19.3 (1983)	11.5	−1.0
25–44	16.4	25.0 (1983)	20.2	+3.8
45+	19.6	32.2 (1985)	28.3	+8.7
Women				
15–24	12.7	17.1 (1983)	11.0	−1.7
25–44	15.4	21.0 (1985)	17.8	+2.4
45+	17.8	26.0 (1986)	21.4	+3.6

Author based on Statistics Canada, 71–529

Men 45 and Over Unemployed for More Than One Year

In contrast to the early part of the decade, a much higher percentage of unemployed men aged 45 and over were off work for more than a year in the second half of the 1980s.

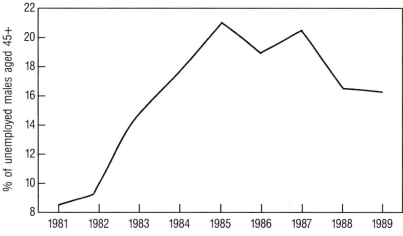

Author based on Statistics Canada, 71–529

People Pattern No. 40
Youth Closing Unemployment Gap

The declining number of youth is working to this group's advantage. Their future should be even better as their numbers will decline further, as outlined in People Pattern 9.

In 1979, the Canadian unemployment rate stood at 7.4 percent; it peaked at 11.8 percent in 1983 and then declined to 7.5 percent in 1989. As such, the total unemployment rate was similar at the beginning and end of the decade.

Using only the unemployment rates for 1979 and 1989, the only winners in relative terms were women aged 15–24 and to a lesser extent men of the same age, who experienced improvements in unemployment rates of 2.6 and 0.8 percentage points respectively. Men aged 25 and over all had higher unemployment rates in 1989 than in 1979. The trends were marginally more positive for women aged 25 and over, with virtually no change for the 25–54 age group and with the only significant increases being for the 55–64 age group.

In more general terms, youth aged 15–24 and to a lesser degree women aged 25 and over have gained in relative terms.

A useful approach to help assess trends in relative positions is to compare age- and sex-specific unemployment rates with the rate for men aged 25 and over. This group is used because it represents what has traditionally been viewed as the "prime wage earner." This relationship is shown on the chart at the bottom of the next page.

In 1979, the 12.9 percent unemployment rate for all youth aged 15–24 was 2.9 times the 4.5 percent unemployment rate for men 25 and over. The ratio improved to 2.3 in 1982 and even further to less than 1.9 in 1989.

The ratio of the female (25 and over) unemployment rate to male (25 and over) unemployment rate suggests that women gained some ground during the recession but have lost some of the advantage in recent years. Women are still relatively better off than during the 1979 to 1981 period. During the 1979 to 1981 period the ratio of female to male unemployment rate was about 1.5 and between 1988 to 1989 the ratio was about 1.2.

And so what . . . The decline in the actual number of youth aged 15–25 has already begun to place this group in an advantageous position relative to the rest of the work force. In time, the relative scarcity of young workers will increase youths' wages as well.

Unemployment Rates by Age and Sex

Unemployment rates for all groups of men 25 years of age and older increased over the last decade.

	1979 (%)	1989 (%)	Change 1979–1987 (%)
TOTAL	7.4	7.5	+0.1
Men			
15–24	13.2	12.4	−0.8
25–34	5.5	7.4	+1.9
35–44	3.9	5.5	+1.6
45–54	4.2	4.8	+0.6
55–64	4.5	6.4	+1.9
TOTAL	6.6	7.3	+0.7
Women			
15–24	12.7	10.1	−2.6
25–34	8.5	8.8	+0.3
35–44	6.8	6.9	+0.1
45–54	6.0	5.9	−0.1
55–64	4.9	6.0	+1.1
TOTAL	8.8	7.9	−0.9

Author based on Statistics Canada, 71–529

Relative Unemployment Rates

The relative unemployment position of youth improved significantly during the 1980s, while the improvement for adult women was less dramatic.

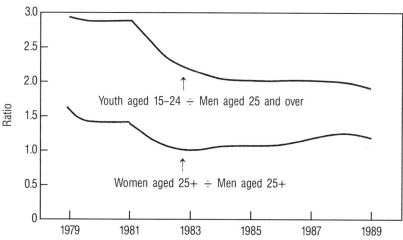

Author based on Statistics Canada, 71–529

People Pattern No. 41
Unemployed Don't Look to Government

The unemployed are looking for new jobs. They are, however, changing the methods they use in the job search.

The vast majority of those who are out of work want to end the situation as soon as possible. During 1989, close to 93 percent of all unemployed Canadians carried on an active search for a new job. Most of those who were not looking were on layoff or were waiting to take up an acquired job within four weeks.

About 9 percent of the unemployed were not actively looking for a new job during the late 1970s. The recession of the early 1980s and the growing uncertainty as to whether the old job would ever return lowered the numbers of those not looking to less than 6 percent. By 1989, it was just above 7 percent.

The most widely used method of finding a new job is contacting prospective employers directly. About 7 out of 10 of the unemployed have used and continue to use this method.

In 1979, the second most used method of job search was contacting a government employment agency. This approach was used by 56 percent of the unemployed. By 1989, however, only 38 percent of those out of work were using government agencies to look for a new job.

At present, the second most popular method of job search is checking the want ads. Slightly more than half of the unemployed use this method compared with less than 40 percent 10 years ago.

And so what . . . Most of the unemployed are not lazy or taking advantage of the system but are actively searching for a way to return to the ranks of the employed. The declining use of government agencies suggests that governments may have to revamp their job-search programs.

Unemployed but Not Looking for Work

The percentage of unemployed Canadians who were not actively looking for work was much lower at the end of the decade than at the beginning.

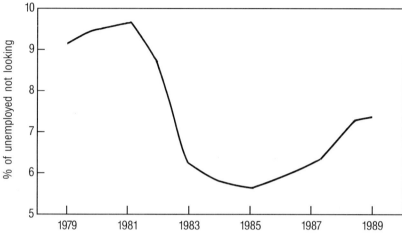

Author based on Statistics Canada, 71–529

Job-Search Methods of the Unemployed

A declining proportion of the unemployed are using government agencies to find a new job.

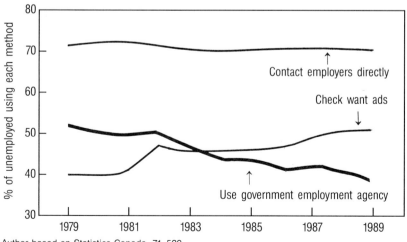

Author based on Statistics Canada, 71–529

TORONTO STAR 19/4/89

Budget could tip many families over the edge

VANCOUVER SUN 9/5/89

TAXING TIMES

Canadians' take-home pay has declined

GLOBE & MAIL Dec. 6/89

Average families' real income unchanged in 1988 from 1980

MONTREAL DAILY NEWS 21/10/88 (also in/aussi dans THE WINNIPEG FREE PRESS 21/10/88 p. 34)

Workers race take-home treadmill

Friday, February 21, 1986   Saskatoon, Saskatchewan   Star-Phoenix

Women working towards equality

FINANCIAL POST 15/3/89

We must address the male/female wage gap

GLOBE & MAIL Jan. 10/90

Women still excluded from training in trades seen as traditionally male

TORONTO STAR 20/3/89

Canada's job gains hide wage losses

FINANCIAL POST Nov. 7/89

Women in banks underpaid: stud

Your Pocketbook:

Bringing Home the "Leaner" Bacon

Throughout the last decade, the headlines reported that Canadians were struggling just to stay afloat financially; they were dead on! The average Canadian family saw its "real" income remain constant throughout the decade as rising prices and increased taxes chewed away at paychecks. This helped create the workaholic family. Unattached individuals fared no better.

If there were any winners during the 1980s, it was the elderly, who saw their incomes rise much faster than the rate of inflation. The losers were single-income couples with children. This helps explain declining fertility rates.

Workers were able to obtain higher fringe benefits during the decade but still ended the decade with lower wages. This has not yet lead to higher wage demands by workers.

The early part of the decade saw women close a small part of the wage gap with men, but for full-time female workers the narrowing stalled during the last half of the decade. This situation will need to be addressed since two-thirds of the jobs created up until the year 2001 will go to women.

All Income Gains Swallowed by Prices and Taxes

If you feel as if it's harder now to make ends meet than it was ten years ago, you are probably correct. Family and individual incomes have barely kept up with inflation over the last decade.

The early 1970s were good for the average Canadian family, with incomes rising rapidly from 1971 to 1976. "Real" gross income before taxes (actual income less price increases) increased by 23 percent during the five-year period. During the last decade, however, progress has been virtually non-existent.

In 1979, the average family brought in $24,245 in "actual" gross income before taxes and deductions. (See the top line of the chart on the next page.) By 1988, the average actual gross income had risen to $46,185. At first glance, this 90 percent increase looks pretty good.

While actual incomes were rising, the prices of the goods and services that could be purchased or rented were also rising. Removing the impact of these increases in prices results in what economists call real gross income. Real gross income of the average family advanced by about 7 percent during the entire 1979 to 1988 period. (See the middle line of the chart.) Don't count your marbles yet, as you still have to pay your income taxes.

In 1987, the average family paid 18.6 percent of gross income in income taxes. This tax payment varied from nil for families with gross incomes of less than $5,000 to 25 percent and over for families with incomes of over $75,000.

After deducting for increases in prices and the impact of taxation, real family incomes rose by less than 1 percent from 1979 to 1987. (See the bottom line of the chart.)

The table on the next page indicates the income changes for unattached individuals have been very similar to those experienced by families.

And so what... The 1980s have not been kind to the average Canadian family or unattached individual, with incomes barely keeping up with inflation and income taxes. This limited gain has maintained the pressure on family budgets and lifestyles. Families have been struggling for more than a decade. The workaholic family may be the result of this financial pressure.

Actual and "Real" Family Incomes

Average family incomes in real terms were stagnant during the last decade as inflation and taxes eroded income gains.

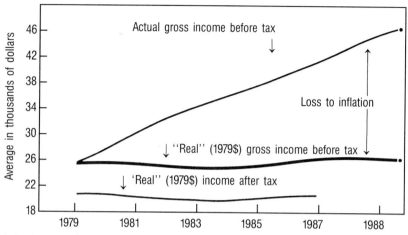

Author based on Statistics Canada, 13–207 and 13–210

Average Income Levels

Neither families nor unattached individuals made much in the way of real income gains during the last decade.

	Per Family		
	1979 ($)	1988 ($)	% Change
Actual Gross Income Before Tax	24,245	46,185	+90.0
"Real" Gross Income Before Tax (1979 Dollars)	24,245	25,882	+6.8
"Real" Income After Tax (1979 Dollars)	20,554	20,735*	+0.9
	Per Unattached Individual		
	1979 ($)	1988 ($)	% Change
Actual Gross Income Before Tax	10,375	19,608	+88.9
"Real" Gross Income Before Tax (1979 Dollars)	10,375	11,006	+6.1
"Real" Income After Tax (1979 Dollars)	8,891	9,030*	+1.6

Author based on Statistics Canada, 13–207 and 13–210
*Refers to 1987

People Pattern No. 43
Elderly Are Winners during the 1980s

The 1980s have been marked by divergent trends in average gross incomes for different types of families and for unattached individuals. The best improvements seem to have been made by those with the lowest income levels.

According to Statistics Canada, the unattached elderly (65 and over) have been the clear winners during the 1980s as their real gross incomes (actual incomes less price increases) before taxes jumped by almost 20 percent over the decade. Notwithstanding the above, this group still had an average annual income of only $14,562 in 1988.

Next in line in terms of income improvements were elderly families, which experienced a 15 percent real gain in incomes from 1979 to 1988. The average gross income of this group was $31,877 in 1988.

Female single-parents who were not working outside the home had a total annual income of just under $11,000 in 1988, despite the fact that the 1980s brought about an 8.7 percent gain in real incomes. The incomes of female single-parents who were working outside the home were higher at $20,649, but registered little real improvement during the 1979 to 1988 period.

Childless, non-elderly married couples (including those in common-law relationships) made real gains during the 1980s, especially among single-income families, which saw real incomes rise by over 10 percent.

What occurred if children were present? Non-elderly married couples (including common-law) with children and three or more earners had the highest average annual incomes of almost $65,000 in 1988, but actually experienced small real income declines from 1979 to 1988. Single-income families also fell behind the rate of inflation. One of the winners in the income game were double-income families with children, who were able to achieve real income gains of about 6 percent and had average family incomes of almost $52,000 in 1988. The proliferation of double-income families is highlighted in People Pattern 32.

Deducting taxes from the above calculations reduces any gains and increases the size of any income declines.

And so what . . . The different relative gains in incomes portrays an ever-changing distribution of the total benefits of the Canadian economy. Policy makers need to continuously assess these trends to ensure that the distribution is fair. The major problem in this respect is that "fairness" is a difficult concept to define and then agree upon.

Average Incomes before Taxes

The decade produced large real income gains for the elderly, while single-income couples with children experienced real income declines.

	Actual Gross Income Before Tax (1988$)	Change 1979–1988 in "Real"[1] Income Before Tax (%)
Per Family (2 or more persons)		
Elderly (Head 65+)	31,877	+14.8
Non-Elderly Married Couples[2] With No Children		
—One Earner	40,168	+10.9
—Two Earners	51,402	+3.1
Non-Elderly Married Couples[2] With Children		
—One Earner	37,351	−1.7
—Two Earners	51,780	+5.6
—Three or More Earners	64,994	−0.5
Non-Elderly Female Single Parent		
—No Earner	10,955	+8.7
—One Earner	20,649	+2.9
Per Unattached Individual		
Elderly (Head 65+)	14,562	+19.3
Non-Elderly	21,569	+2.5

Author based on Statistics Canada, 13–207
[1] Change after removing impact of higher prices.
[2] Married includes common-law unions.

People Pattern No. 44

More Benefits Not Enough
to Compensate for Wage Losses

The most important source of income for the average Canadian is paid employment. Paid workers have struggled to keep up with inflation throughout the 1980s but have failed.

The income measure used in this People Pattern includes gross wages and salaries before deductions plus any supplementary benefits such as employers' contributions to health and welfare schemes, pension plans, workers' compensation, and unemployment insurance funds. The estimates include both full- and part-time workers.

In 1987, the average annual wage and benefit package was worth $27,900 per individual worker in Canada. This varied from a low of $12,600 for workers in primary sectors (agriculture, fishing, and trapping) to a high of $41,600 for paid workers in mining.

The income of the average worker declined by about 1 percent in "real" terms from 1979 to 1987 (that is, after removing the impact of inflation). The changes from 1979 to 1987 in "real" labour income per worker varied sharply, with declines of over 12 percent in the primary sectors to an average gain of over 18 percent in the finance, insurance, and real estate sectors.

In 1987, the total wage and benefit package per worker was comprised of $25,200 in wages and salaries and $2,700 in benefits. Between 1979 and 1987, the real wage and salary actually declined by 2.3 percent per worker and benefits registered a real improvement of 8 percent. As seen earlier, the combination of both the wage and benefit sides resulted in a real loss overall. Benefits rose from 7.8 percent of wages and salaries in 1979 to 10.7 percent in 1987.

And so what . . . The decline in real incomes for the average worker represents a break in a much longer trend of rising incomes. So far, this negative trend has not lead to significantly higher wage demands from workers. If wage gains do not resume, the number of hours workers are putting in (on a main job or on a second job) will need to increase further and the number of workers per family will also need to increase. The workaholic household will become an even more established feature of Canadian life.

Average Annual Income per Paid Worker

Paid workers in finance, insurance, and real estate made healthy gains in real incomes during the years 1979 to 1987.

	Actual Income Before Tax 1987	"Real"* % Change 1979–1987
Goods Producing Industries	$31,300	+2.6
Primary	$12,600	−12.5
Forestry	$37,600	−10.7
Mining	$41,600	+0.2
Manufacturing	$31,800	+7.4
Construction	$32,100	−4.1
Service Producing Industries	$26,700	−2.2
Transportation, Communication and Other Utilities	$35,500	+5.0
Wholesale and Retail Trade	$20,900	−4.1
Finance, Insurance and Real Estate	$35,500	+18.3
Community, Business and Personal Service	$25,000	−4.2
Government	$31,300	−1.9
All Industries	$27,900	−1.1

Author based on Statistics Canada, 71–001

Note: Average annual income includes wages and salaries and supplementary benefits such as employers' contributions to health and welfare, sickness, pension plans, workers' compensation, and unemployment insurance funds.
 * Change after removing impact of higher prices.

Average "Real" Income per Worker

Worker fringe benefits rose from under 8 percent to almost 11 percent of income over the period 1979 to 1987.

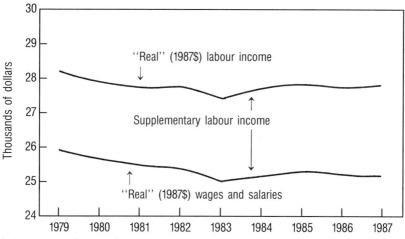

Author based on Statistics Canada, 71–001

Women's Earnings Catching Up Very Slowly

One of the major challenges facing Canadian society is to eliminate the inequality of men's and women's earnings. The challenge is very important since two-thirds of all the workers who will join the labour force between now and the year 2001 will be women.

In 1988, the average woman working full-time for a full year (50–52 weeks) earned $21,918; the average man working full-time for a year earned $33,558. This 65 percent female to male earnings ratio for 1988 represents a slow improvement from 58 percent in 1967 and 62 percent in 1977 but repesents no improvement at all from 1984.

In the group of all other workers (part-timers or permanent for less than a full year), the average woman earned $7,991 and the average man earned $10,735. This results in a much higher female to male ratio of 75 percent. This "all other worker" female to male earnings ratio has moved up sharply from around 50 percent in 1977 and 63 percent in 1983. The reasons for this improvement are not yet evident.

Differentials are smallest for younger workers. In 1988, full-year, full-time female workers aged 15–24 earned 84 percent of what males earned, with the gap worsening to 72 percent for the 25–34 age group and to near 60 percent for all others.

Single (never-married) women earned 90 percent of what single men earned, in contrast to a ratio of 61 percent when the comparison is between married women and married men.

Higher levels of education have tended to narrow wage differences among full-year, full-time workers. The female to male earnings ratio is 57 percent for those with some or all of a high school education, compared with 72 percent for those with a university education. Similar conclusions are evident in People Pattern 15. In addition, women have increased their share within each one of the 46 major professional categories in Canada (categories in which 45 percent or more of the employed have at least a bachelor's degree). The entry of more women into traditionally male-dominated jobs is helping to narrow the wage gap.

And so what . . . The female to male wage disadvantage should continue to narrow as women increase their presence in all occupations, further improve their educational levels, move into full-time, full-year employment, and as both men and women get rid of outdated myths. Pay equity and female promotion programs will need to be strengthened to narrow the disadvantage more quickly because it seems that the narrowing has stalled in recent years.

Ratios of Female to Male Earnings by Year

Women in full-time, full-year jobs improved their position relative to men until 1984, when they stalled.

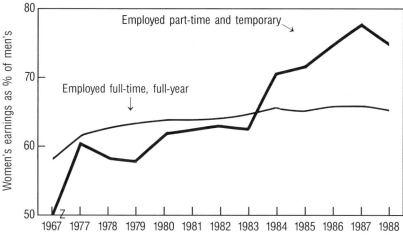

Author based on Statistics Canada, 13–217

Ratios of Female to Male Earnings by Age Group

Earnings of younger women are much closer to those of men than is the case for older groups.

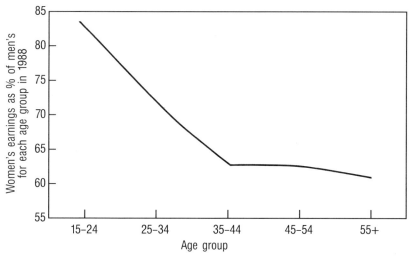

Author based on Statistics Canada, 13–217
Note: Includes only people employed full-time, full year.

The Toronto Star, Nov. 16/89

A search for the root causes of poverty

Two-year study aims to find better ways to break poverty cycle

Middle-class Canadians take the heat

MONTREAL GAZETTE 10/3/89

NFB films zero in on why women are poor

Montreal Gazette 8/6/89
(Also in/aussi dans Le Devoir 8/

Old-age pensions rise in July

OTTAWA CITIZEN
13/4/89

'Grocery stores of the poor'

**Food bank
volunteers
says govt.
shirking duties**

Winnipeg Free Press 16/06/89

Single parents' poverty decried

The GLOBE & MAIL Dec. 30/89

Women ride roller-coaster of hope, despair

The GLOBE & MAIL Nov. 24/89

Reichmann, me and the vanishing middle class

The GLOBE & MAIL Dec. 19/89

CANADA NEWS 13/1/89

Five million poor Canadians

Minimum wages fail to improve lot of working poor, group says

Poverty, Wealth, and the Middle Class:

The Prospering Seniors and the Struggling Single-Income Family

Money and how it is distributed is an issue often discussed in the media. Money is very important to Canadians.

Over 3.3 million Canadians live in poverty with over one-quarter being children. The number of people living in poverty rose during the recession-depression of the early 1980s but has been declining since then. Over the decade, impressive gains were made by the elderly, for whom poverty rates were reduced sharply. Single parents and single-income families with children experienced increases in poverty.

The richest 20 percent of Canadian households are taking in a growing portion of annual incomes and control almost 70 percent of all household wealth. In contrast, the poorest 40 percent of households control less than 2 percent of the total wealth. The middle class is shrinking while the better off are gaining. An easy-to-use "age-income" matrix shows you where you fit in the income rankings.

The accumulation of wealth takes time. Average household wealth climbs slowly for young households, peaks at $137,000 for households with a head aged 55–64, and then begins to decline. The increased equity in homes is the source of much of the wealth accumulation.

People Pattern No. 46
Poverty Is High but Declining

The amount of income that a person or family needs to just "get by" is widely debated. In Canada there are many different approaches used to estimate poverty rates. Statistics Canada uses the less emotive term "low-income" and "straitened circumstances" to measure what most people call poverty; the terms are interchangeable.

According to Statistics Canada, individuals or families that spend more than 58.5 percent of their gross incomes on food, shelter, and clothing are considered to be low-income.

In 1988, 10.5 percent of all Canadian families were classified as low-income, down from over 13 percent in 1979. A reduction in low-income rates was also evident for unattached individuals, where low income declined from over 40 percent in 1979 to 33 percent in 1988.

The 3.3 million Canadians now living in poverty compares with over 4 million during both 1983 and 1984. The 875,000 Canadian children under the age of 16 living in poverty in 1988 was at its lowest level since 1980: the number of poor children had been above 1 million during each of 1982, 1983, 1984, and 1985.

The lower number of low-income Canadians has been mostly due to very significant financial improvements among the elderly aged 65 and over. In 1979, 22 percent of elderly families were living in poverty. This ratio fell to 8 percent by 1988. The low-income ratio for elderly unattached individuals declined from over 66 percent in 1979 to under 40 percent in 1988.

Single-parent families headed by women are the worst hit by poverty. In both 1979 and 1988, about 95 percent of single-parent families headed by a woman with no employment earnings lived in poverty. Almost half of the families where the mother was working also lived in poverty.

The incidence of low-income among non-elderly married couples with children increased slightly for two out of three groups. The biggest deterioration was among single-income families, with 17 percent of these families living in poverty in 1988 compared with 16 percent in 1979.

And so what . . . The high incidence of poverty among single-income married couples with children and female single-parent households suggests that the present and future of many children is bleak. It also points to fewer children in the future. Programs to help break the poverty cycle are essential if child poverty is to be reduced significantly.

Incidence of Poverty

Poverty rates declined during the decade, even if a spike occurred due to the recession of the early 1980s.

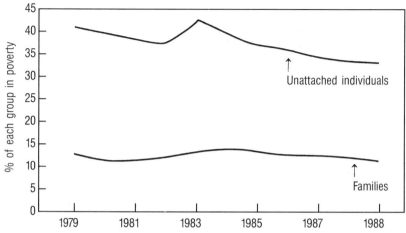

Author based on Statistics Canada, 13–207

Incidence of Poverty in Families and Unattached Individuals

Poverty rates declined sharply among the elderly, but rose for single-income couples with children.

	Incidence of Poverty[1]	
	1979 (%)	1988 (%)
Families (2 or more persons)	13.1	10.5
Elderly (Head 65+)	21.9	8.1
Non-Elderly Married Couples[2] With No Children		
—One Earner	11.0	8.7
—Two Earners	2.0	2.3
Non-Elderly Married Couples[2] With Children		
—One Earner	16.0	17.1
—Two Earners	5.5	5.3
—Three or More Earners	2.3	2.8
Non-Elderly Female Single Parent		
—No Earner	95.9	94.0
—One Earner	45.9	44.3
Unattached Individuals	40.3	33.1
Elderly (Head 65+)	66.3	38.8
Non-Elderly	30.2	30.9

Author based on Statistics Canada, 13–207

[1] 58.5% of income spent on food, clothing and shelter.
[2] Married includes common-law unions.

People Pattern No. 47

The Attack on the Middle Class?

The comment is often heard that Canada "is losing its middle class." This comment is directionally correct as the upper-income groups are gaining in position. A key fact in Canada is that incomes and wealth remain very unevenly distributed.

One way to think about the question of income distribution is to imagine that it is possible to line up (from low to high) all Canadian households according to the income received in a given year. Start with the poorest household in Canada (it could be an individual or a family) and move up the line until you have 40 percent of the households; call this group the poorest 40 percent. The next 40 percent of households you can classify as the middle 40 percent, or middle class. The remaining households (who all have more income than the households already selected) are the richest 20 percent. This results in three income classes. To obtain the distribution for accumulated wealth, the process would begin by lining up all households according to how much wealth each has accumulated and then proceeding as above.

Since 1979, the poorest 40 percent of Canadian households have received about 16 percent of the total income generated each year. The richest 20 percent of households have seen their share rise from 41 percent of all income in 1979 to over 42 percent in 1988. The middle 40 percent group lost ground in that its share fell from 43 percent in 1979 to 42 percent in 1988.

When the measurement relates to "accumulated wealth," the distribution is even more unequal, with the poorest 40 percent of households in 1984 holding on to only 1.7 percent of all the wealth in Canada. The share of the wealth held by the middle 40 percent fluctuated around 29 to 30 percent during 1970 to 1984. The share of all wealth held by the richest 20 percent of households declined between 1970 and 1977 and then increased again. The wealthiest 20 percent now hold on to almost 70 percent of all the personal wealth in Canada.

And so what . . . The very uneven distribution of income and wealth in Canada is a reality that troubles many Canadians. The latest patterns do not point to any reversal of long-term trends and thus the issue will continue to be hotly debated.

Total Annual Income by Class

The richest 20 percent of households made a small relative income gain at the expense of the middle class.

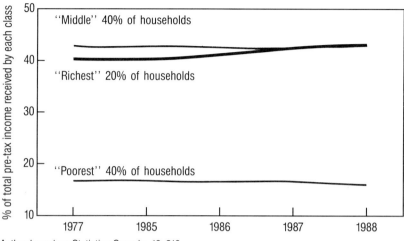

Author based on Statistics Canada, 13–216

Total Accumulated Wealth by Class

Little change is evident in the very unequal distribution of wealth among Canadian households.

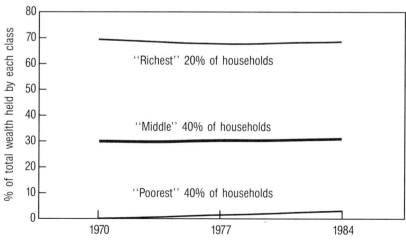

Author based on Statistics Canada, 13–588

People Pattern No. 48
You and the Age-Income Matrix

The age-income matrix on the next page is a useful and simple way to examine income distribution. It can also be used to study how households spend or save their money.

You can easily find yourself in such a matrix by locating the age of the head of your household and the gross income received within your household in 1988. A household can be either a family or an unattached individual. According to Statistics Canada, only one "head" can exist in any household. (You decide!)

For example, find the cell representing a household with the head aged 45–54 that received a gross income of $35,000–44,999 in 1988. This household was one of 215,000 households in this situation in 1988. These households constituted 2.3 percent of all Canadian households.

The totals on the far right of the rows indicate how many households are in each of the income categories listed on the left, and the totals at the bottom of the columns indicate how many households are in each age group shown at the top. The largest number of households by age are headed by people under 35 (2,668,000 households), and the largest income category is $35,000–44,900, earned by 1,342,000 households.

The age-income matrix indicates that most households in the $35,000–44,999 income category are headed by people under 35 years old. For those aged 35–64, most households had incomes of over $70,000 in 1988. For the 65 and over age group, the largest income category was $10,000–14,999.

The use of the age-income matrix enables a more specific analysis of households and markets and where you stand. Just find your age and income and then compare.

And so what... The age-income matrix has been used by large organizations such as department stores to isolate and measure the markets they are trying to serve. The matrix can be used to measure penetration of a whole variety of products, such as microwave ovens and home computers. (See People Pattern 57.) It is also an easy way to compare yourself with your neighbours.

Thousands of Households Within Each "Age-Income" Cell

Households headed by people under 35 and with incomes of $35,000 to $44,999 form the largest single group in Canada.

1988 Household Income Group	Age of Head of Household					
	Under 35	35–44	45–54	55–64	65+	TOTAL
Under $10,000	231	110	79	154	277	851
$10,000–14,999	202	77	62	106	406	854
$15,000–19,999	238	98	64	98	351	850
$20,000–24,999	227	126	90	106	187	736
$25,000–29,999	248	139	76	107	128	698
$30,000–34,999	255	165	91	105	98	714
$35,000–44,999	463	342	215	181	141	1,342
$45,000–54,999	353	341	211	142	81	1,128
$55,000–69,999	270	342	263	141	62	1,078
$70,000+	182	388	364	225	67	1,226
TOTAL	2,668	2,130	1,515	1,365	1,799	9,477

Author based on Statistics Canada, 13–218

Household Wealth Takes Time

Almost all young adults and the not so young complain about tight budgets, and the difficulty of paying off debt and building up savings. Patience seems to be the key.

Collecting data on total wealth accumulation by households is not an easy task and has only been attempted three times during the last two decades. The latest Statistics Canada study refers to the year 1984 and is based on a survey of 14,000 Canadian households. The difficulties relate to the fact that most people hold this type of information "close to the chest" and that a very high level of detailed information is required for both assets and debt. Most of these numbers would be higher if they were measured today.

The average value of assets of a household headed by a person under 25 years of age is a little above $14,000. The value of total assets rises to $60,000 by ages 25–34, to $107,000 by ages 35–44, to $142,000 by 45–54, and peaks at $144,000 by 55–64. Total assets decline after the age of 65.

Up until the age of 65, the fastest growing asset is the home in which the householder lives. Other fixed assets (such as cars, trucks, other real estate, etc.) increase slowly and peak for households aged 55–64. The value of liquid assets (such as cash and Canada Savings Bonds) seems to grow very slowly until the ages of 35–44 but then rise quickly to $25,000 by the age of 65. Other financial assets such as stocks and RRSPs increase slowly as households age.

But how much do you owe? The average value of debt taken on by households under 25 years of age is about $5,500, which then rises to a peak of $21,000 for households aged 35–44. Total debt subsequently declines to only $1,200 for the 65 and over group.

The difference between average assets and average debt provides a rough estimate of average household "wealth" or net worth. Average household wealth peaks at $137,000 for households aged 55–64 before it begins to decline.

And so what . . . The majority of households build up their asset base gradually as they grow older, with most maintaining high debt levels into their mid-forties. This pattern suggests that savings will rise and borrowing will decline as the age structure matures into the next century. This will lead to lower interest rates as savings surge, and could bring about a boom in business investment in the face of labour shortages.

Average Value of Wealth by Age

The highest average wealth (assets minus debt) of almost $140,000 is reached by households headed by people aged 55–64.

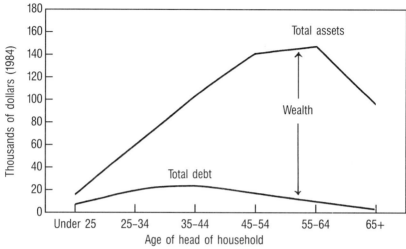

Author based on special tabulation by Statistics Canada

Average Wealth Accumulated by Households Within Each "Age-Income" Cell

The wealthiest households, at $417,981, are headed by people aged 65 and over who still earn over $50,000 a year in income.

1984 Household Income Group	Age of Head of Household					
	Under 25	25–34	35–44	45–54	55–64	65+
	$					
Under $20,000	5,615	19,546	40,248	49,484	65,172	52,033
$20,000–29,999	11,738	34,317	58,559	90,238	107,265	144,497
$30,000–39,999	21,902	44,237	71,590	106,393	138,802	171,500
$40,000–49,999	N/A	52,790	87,565	145,061	174,782	214,709
$50,000 and over	N/A	128,176	178,307	233,226	298,372	417,981

Author based on special tabulation by Statistics Canada
Note: "Average wealth" means total assets minus total debt.

GLOBE & MAIL Dec. 28/89

1990s consumer will be a chubby abstainer

VANCOUVER PROVINCE 14/10/88

SALES ARE UP

FINANCIAL POST 27/2/89

Living cost almost doubles in 10 years

he Toronto Star 13/05/89

Consumers less willing to buy big-ticket items

MONTREAL GAZETTE 10/6/89

Canadians are slowing down their rate of borrowing

TORONTO STAR 22/2/89

Yule spendfest brightens year for retailers

Saskatoon, Saskatchewan Star-Phoenix Thursday, December 14, 1989

'Don't pay a cent till Lent' mentality

THE TORONTO STAR, NOV. 12/89

Save, pay debts as economic sky darkens, forecasters say

GLOBE & MAIL 15/2/89

Costs of yuppie lifestyle to gain official status

You Earned It...
Now Spend It:

The Couch Potato and the Decline of Vice

Together, Canadians earn and then distribute over half a trillion dollars throughout the economy. The patterns of expenditures have changed significantly over time.

After removing the impact of inflation and taxes, real spending still increased over the last decade. Consumers have played their part in keeping the economy moving.

The different pace of price increases seems to have been a key factor in encouraging the growth of the "couch potato," as the price of home entertainment items rose much less than the costs of entertainment outside the home.

The fastest growing expenditure items mirror the needs of an increasing number of double-income families and singles. Real expenditures on "vices" declined during the decade: spending on both alcoholic beverages and tobacco products decreased as prices of these items soared during the decade.

Low-income households spend large portions of available funds on necessities. Households with higher incomes spend more money on clothing, recreation, entertainment, books, and taxes.

People Pattern No. 50
The Circle of Earning and Spending

Canadians have over half a trillion dollars of income to distribute among governments, savings, and purchases of goods and services. Credit and savings help even out the flow.

Total personal income of individuals in Canada rose from $220 billion in 1979 to over $550 billion in 1989. This adds up to an increase of 150 percent during the decade.

The increasing role of government in the lives of Canadians is easy to see in dollar terms. Transfers to governments (income taxes, unemployment premiums, property taxes, etc.) have almost tripled, increasing from about $40 billion in 1979 to about $120 billion in 1989.

After transfers to government, consumers had roughly $430 billion of personal disposable income in 1989. During the 1979 to 1989 period, personal disposable income increased by 140 percent.

Individual Canadians put away $23 billion in 1979. Annual savings increased to above $40 billion during the recession period as unemployment and uncertainty caused consumers to retrench. Savings subsequently declined in 1986 and 1987 before rising again to reach $44 billion by 1989.

Consumer and mortgage credit continued to rise significantly throughout the decade, even if the recession did cause the pace of credit expansion to slow. It accelerated again to 1989. Canadians ended the decade with high debt loads.

The actual dollar value of consumer expenditures rose from $153 billion in 1979 to over $380 billion in 1989, or by almost 150 percent.

The majority of the expenditure increase was due to inflation. After removing the impact of higher prices, the real volume of spending advanced by a much smaller 37 percent.

And so what . . . The earning, spending, borrowing, and saving of incomes is what the Canadian economy is really all about. The simple circle of earning and spending is intertwined with governments and international trade. The educational system must place a higher emphasis on teaching the workings of the system.

Distribution of Personal Income

Individuals earn income, transfer some to government, put a bit away in savings, and spend the rest.

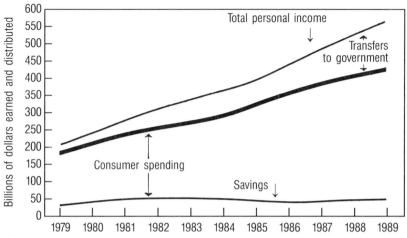

Author based on Statistics Canada, 13–001

Actual and "Real" Consumer Spending

Actual consumer spending increased by almost 150 percent during the decade, but in real terms amounted to a smaller, but significant, 37 percent advance.

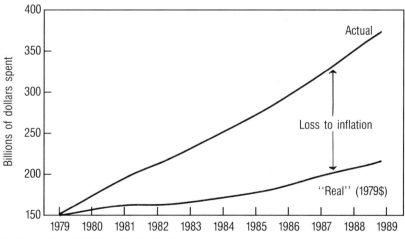

Author based on Statistics Canada, 13–001

127

People Pattern No. 51
Consumer Prices and the Couch Potato

Unemployment and consumer prices are the two most widely reported economic indicators in Canada. Consumer prices have increased every year but one during the second half of the twentieth century.

The consumer price index measures the change in the price of a "basket" of goods and services purchased by consumers. The early 1980s were marked by price inflation in the double-digit range, with the single year peak in 1982 at 12.5 percent. The 1984 to 1988 period evidenced price hikes of about 4 percent each year. Inflation has now moved back into the 5 percent area.

Over the entire 1979 to 1989 period, the price of the total consumer basket advanced by 87 percent. As seen in People Patterns 42 to 44, inflation has just about wiped out gains in family incomes and has surpassed the increase in wages and benefits per worker.

The change in prices of individual items within the basket of goods and services has varied greatly. The largest increase for an item has been the more than tripling (+259 percent) in the price of tobacco supplies, and the smallest increase (+16 percent) has been in the price of home entertainment items.

The price of food has risen with the cost of food consumed at home (+71 percent) increasing less than food consumed away from home (+82 percent). Home ownership costs (+94 percent) rose more quickly than rental costs (+69 percent). Clothing prices all rose within a rather narrow range of 58 to 62 percent.

Very large increases have occurred for both alcoholic beverages (+133 percent) and public transportation costs (+135 percent).

The price of goods (+84 percent) has risen somewhat less than the price of services (+91 percent).

And so what... Relative price hikes help consumers decide which goods and services to buy. The major difference between the price of admission to events (including movies) versus the cost of home entertainment items has played a significant role in the rise of the "couch potato." Sellers of products and services should always remember that most consumers watch their budgets and in the long run high-priced items lose out to lower-priced items.

Annual Consumer Prices

Inflation entered the decade with annual double-digit hikes and ended with increases of 4 to 5 percent.

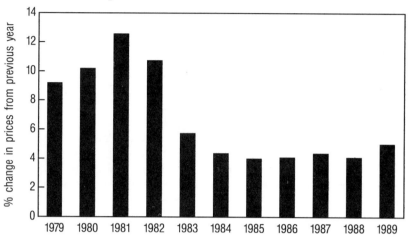

Author based on Statistics Canada, 62–001

Consumer Price Changes During the Decade

Price increases during the 1980s ranged from a high of 259 percent for tobacco supplies to a low of 16 percent for home entertainment items.

	Change 1979–1989 (%)		Change 1979–1989 (%)
TOTAL Price Changes	+87	**Health and Personal Care**	
Food		Health Care	+109
Food at Home	+71	Personal Care	+70
Food Away from Home	+82	**Recreation and Reading**	
Housing		Admission to Events	+114
Ownership	+94	Home Entertainment	+16
Rental Accommodation	+69	Recreation Equipment	+57
Household Operation	+75	Reading	+121
Clothing			
Men's	+58	**Tobacco and Alcohol**	
Women's	+62	Tobacco Supplies	+259
Girls' Wear	+59	Alcoholic Beverages	
Boys' Wear	+58	from Stores	+133
Transportation		**Goods**	+84
Private Transportation	+96		
Public Transportation	+135	**Services**	+91

Author based on Statistics Canada, 62–010

People Pattern No. 52
Fewer Purchases of "Vices"

Consumers use their disposable dollars to buy goods and services. The direction in which these dollars go has changed during the last decade.

The following table summarizes the expenditures by consumers in 1988 along with the change over the last decade in actual dollars and in real dollars (after removal of price increases). The categories are listed according to the percentage size of the real growth registered during the last decade, as shown in the last column.

In actual dollar terms, the largest expenditure category is the cost of home ownership at over $45 billion, followed by the purchase of food and non-alcoholic beverages at about $40 billion. Next are expenditures in restaurants and hotels at $23 billion and the purchase of new and used motor vehicles at almost $20 billion.

The pattern of real growth is revealing. At the top is the 112 percent increase in real expenditures on recreation, sporting, and camping equipment. A close second is the growth in domestic and child-care expenses. Communications, toilet articles, cosmetics, and motor vehicle repair are all next in line. All of these expenditures are consistent with the needs of a growing number of busy double-income families and singles with a need to commute, communicate, clean, care, and relax.

The next five fastest growing categories are basic housing, personal care, drugs and sundries, and recreational services.

At the very bottom of the list are the "vices" that have been taxed heavily and publicly scorned. Drinking and smoking are no longer cool as these are the only two categories that have experienced real declines during the last decade.

And so what . . . The goods and services purchased by consumers reflect relative prices, the satisfaction of basic needs, and the changing structure of households. This is what *Canadian People Patterns* is really all about: our patterns reflect and measure our changing lifestyles.

Personal Spending on Consumer Goods and Services, Including Taxes

Alcoholic beverages and tobacco products were the only two major categories of spending to experience real declines during the 1980s.

	Expenditures 1988	% Change 1979–1988	
	Millions $	Actual	"Real" *
Recreation, Sporting and Camping Equipment	14,018	159	112
Domestic and Child Services	3,769	250	106
Communications	5,677	132	73
Toilet Articles, Cosmetics	3,361	178	72
Motor Vehicle Repair and Parts	8,164	156	67
Household Appliances	5,384	119	57
Personal Care	3,031	165	54
Housing Ownership Costs	45,461	154	50
Drugs and Sundries	5,061	202	50
Recreational Services	9,400	189	48
Natural Gas	2,536	156	46
Gross Rent Paid	16,957	144	41
New and Used Motor Vehicles	19,459	138	41
Medical Care	7,077	167	37
Education and Cultural Services	9,479	112	35
Electricity	6,819	164	30
Non-durable Household Supplies	7,241	131	28
Financial, Legal, Other Services	17,260	157	28
Semi-durable Household Furnishings	9,256	108	27
Jewelry, Watches and Repair	2,278	74	26
Men's and Boys' Clothing	7,204	91	25
Women's and Children's Clothing	10,135	92	22
Reading and Entertainment Supplies	6,014	119	18
Footwear and Repair	3,003	82	17
Furniture, Carpets, Other Floor Coverings	5,358	84	16
Expenditures on Restaurants and Hotels	22,627	111	16
Food and Non-Alcoholic Beverages	39,749	89	14
Purchased Transportation	6,892	130	14
Laundry and Dry Cleaning	999	103	10
Motor Fuels and Lubricants	10,675	122	3
Alcoholic Beverages	10,137	110	−6
Tobacco Products	7,287	152	−18

Author based on Statistics Canada, 63–531
* Change after removing impact of higher prices

People Pattern No. 53
Less Food and More Taxes as Incomes Rise

Acquire the basics and then move up when incomes allow. This pattern describes the reality for the majority of Canadian households. Higher incomes lead to higher expenditures on less-basic items and services and to much higher taxes.

Nothing is more basic than food. In 1986, the typical household spent about $5,000 on food, or 14 percent of total household expenditures. Households with incomes under $10,000 spent about one-quarter of their income on food compared with about 11 percent for households with annual incomes above $60,000. Eating out is less basic, with the best-off households spending one-third of their larger food budgets in restaurants compared with only 13 percent spent in restaurants by the lower income households.

Food and then shelter. While the average family spends about 16 percent of its income on the provision of basic shelter, households at the low end of the income scale spend one-third on shelter. The $60,000 and over crowd spend only 12 percent.

Wealthier households also spend a smaller percent of their total household income on household operation, health and personal care (not plotted), and tobacco and alcohol.

While the share of total income spent on the above falls for better-off households, the actual dollar amount spent on each of these items rises as income rises. For example, households with an annual income of less than $10,000 spend about $3,000 on shelter, and households with an annual income of more than $60,000 spend over $9,000.

As incomes increase, expenditures on clothing, recreation, entertainment, and books rise slowly as a percent of total expenditures. Excluding households with incomes of less than $15,000, transportation expenditures consume a fairly constant share of incomes.

Personal taxes rise sharply as household income rises.

And so what ... Income is the key determinant of economic well being. Concerned individuals and society as a whole are working to ensure that low-income Canadians can at least acquire the basics with some hope of bettering their lifestyle. Many higher income Canadians will continue to complain about personal taxes.

Makeup of Spending

As incomes rise, a smaller percentage of incomes go for shelter and food, with a larger proportion allocated to taxes.

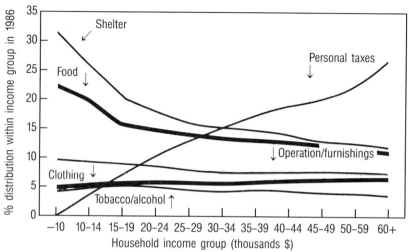

Author based on Statistics Canada, 62–555

Food Spending

Rising incomes lead to rapidly rising expenditures in restaurants and other eating places.

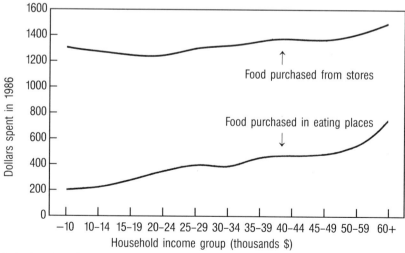

Author based on Statistics Canada, 62–555

Higher incomes means nicer kitchens

The Leader-Post

Regina, Saskatchewan

Monday, April 9, 1984

TORONTO STAR 3/6/89

The electronic family

The Globe and Mail, Nov. 7/89
Also in/aussi dans The Ottawa Citizen, Nov. 5/89

Canadians turned on by home electronics

The Toronto Star 25/05/

The Toronto Star, Nov. 16/89

Wealth of new products target future decade of health, fitness

More of us lead active lifestyles study finds

VANCOUVER SUN 8/10/88

Personal computers invade Canadian homes as '80s high-tech tool of all trades

TORONTO STAR 10/10/88

What were once thought luxuries are now necessities, figures show

MONTREAL GAZETTE 10/3/90 P. A7 also in/aussi dans
GLOBE & MAIL 10/3/89 P. B5

Poor buying more VCRs, microwaves

OTTAWA CITIZEN 28/5/89

As CD, cassette sales soar, vinyl given another 5 years

MONTREAL GAZETTE 6/4/89

More Canadians buying 2nd cars

Fulfillment:

Paying Off the Mortgage and the "Good Life"

A home with plenty of comforts is the goal of most Canadians. The public press is continually tracking the gains.

Householders rent when they are young and rent again when they are old. "Paying-off the mortgage" parties become popular as individuals reach the age of 45.

The average Canadian home is getting more comfortable and is filling up with home entertainment items and gadgets. A clear majority of homes now have smoke detectors, clothes dryers, and freezers, and the ownership of microwaves is soaring. On the entertainment side, virtually every home now has a colour TV, the vast majority have two or more radios, a cassette recorder, and cable TV. VCR ownership is increasing rapidly.

The ownership of all comfort and entertainment gadgets rises sharply as household incomes rise. The view that low-income families spend too much money on items they do not need is not substantiated by the facts.

The age-income matrix first discussed in People Pattern 48 reveals that low-income households under age 35 are most likely to be renters. Those most likely to be owners have incomes of at least $70,000 and have heads aged 55–64. Use the age-income matrix to see where you stand.

People Pattern No. 54

To Rent or to Own?

While all Canadians have a pride of ownership, it seems that income and age play a major role in determining whether to rent or own.

The choice between ownership and renting of accommodations is strongly influenced by income levels. Recent data (1989) reveal that 70 percent of all housholds with incomes under $10,000 per year are renters. The percentage of renters declines gradually with rising household incomes, with only 12 percent of the highest income group being renters.

A strong relationship exists between incomes and the probability that home owners have mortgages, with the relationship being the opposite of what might be expected. Fewer than 10 percent of households with incomes less than $10,000 have home mortgages, but over 50 percent of households with incomes over $70,000 have home mortgages. More income suggests a greater ability to support mortgage payments, which in turn encourages people to borrow and encourages the financial institutions to satisfy them.

About 30 to 40 percent of all but one income group own a home without a mortgage. The exception is the lowest income group, where only one-quarter own a home without a mortgage.

Age is another major factor that determines living accommodations. Six out of every 10 householders who are less than 35 years of age are renters. Renters as a percent of total householders decline to a low of about 25 percent for the 45–64 age group and then rise again for householders aged 65 years and over.

As might be expected, the older the household the more likely the mortgage has been paid off. By the age of 45–54, about one-third of households have been able to pay off their home mortgages. By the age of 55 and over, at least 60 percent of households have mortgage-free homes.

And so what . . . The aging population will increase the demand for rental units or at least the demand for smaller homes. Higher disposable incomes will also increase as households are freed from the mortgage burden. Older Canadians will be the boom market for marketers as Canada enters the twenty-first century.

Home Ownership by Income Group

Lower income households are more likely to rent their homes.

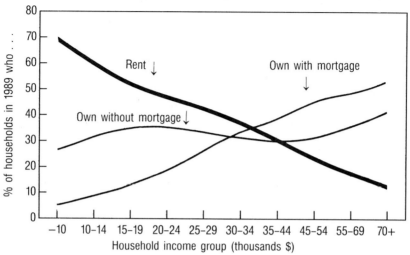

Author based on Statistics Canada, 13–218

Home Ownership by Age Group

At least 60 percent of households with the head aged 55 have paid off their mortgages.

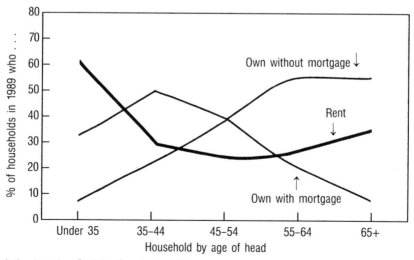

Author based on Statistics Canada, 13–218

People Pattern No. 55
The Gadgets that Make a Home

While home may be "where the heart is," it is also much more in terms of the comfort and entertainment items that fill it. The modern home is designed for convenience and efficiency.

Certain "home comfort" items make the home a safer and more efficient place live. On the safety side, more than 8 out of every 10 homes now have a smoke detector. When the smoke detector goes off, however, less than half of Canadian households are equipped with a fire extinguisher. Air conditioners are more popular but are still found in only 25 percent of homes.

Doing the laundry is much easier than it used to be, with over 70 percent of all households now having access to both an automatic washing machine and a clothes dryer. Work in the kitchen is also much simpler, with over 40 percent of households now using an automatic dishwasher, 63 percent using a microwave oven, and 58 percent having a freezer.

The number of households with two or more cars has remained near 25 percent for a decade. More vans and trucks are evident.

"Couch potatoes" have colourful entertainment at the push of a button. Ninety-six percent of households now have at least one colour television; over 75 percent of households have two or more radios, 70 percent have cassette recorders and cable television, and almost 60 percent own video recorders (VCRs). Still bored? Virtually all households have a telephone and over one-third have three or more telephones. About 13 percent of households have a home computer.

Only 6 out of every 100 households have a vacation home.

And so what... The modern home enables tasks to be performed faster and more efficiently than ever before and has a home entertainment centre offering a wide variety of items. This revolution is having an impact on family dynamics and community relationships in ways that are still not appreciated.

Change in Ownership of "Home Comfort" Items

Microwave ovens and smoke detectors made the sharpest advances in Canadian homes.

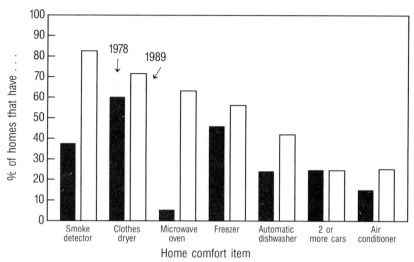

Author based on Statistics Canada, 13–218

Change in Ownership of "Home Entertainment" Items

Virtually non-existent in 1978, VCRs are now in 60 percent of Canadian homes.

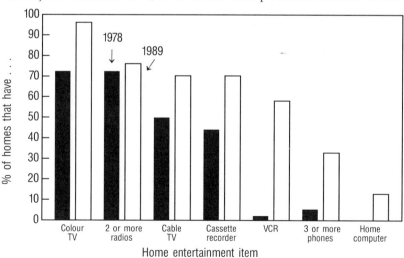

Author based on Statistics Canada, 13–218

Money Means Comfort

The ownership of home comfort and home entertainment items has increased significantly over the last decade. Household income seems to be the key factor determining which households modernize first.

The chart at the top of the next page gives one very clear message. Money buys material items to help perform both necessary tasks and provide entertainment!

The percentage of homes with clothes dryers is just under 45 percent for households with incomes of less than $10,000 and over 90 percent for households with incomes of $70,000 or more.

The impact of incomes is even more dramatic with respect to ownership of video recorders (VCRs), microwave ovens, and automatic dishwashers. For each of these items, the ownership rate is 72 to 82 percent for households with incomes of $70,000 or more and 15 to 30 percent for households at the low end of the income scale.

Households with incomes of $70,000 and over are three times more likely to own a home computer than are households with incomes between $30,000 and $35,000 and six times more likely to own a home computer than are households with incomes of under $10,000.

Age is another important factor which determines rate of ownership. For every item, peak ownership is achieved within households with heads aged 35–54 years. Among older households, the "high-tech" items such as VCRs and home computers are much less popular than are more practical items such as microwaves and clothes dryers.

And so what . . . The statement is often made that poor families do not know how to budget and that they spend their incomes on items thay cannot afford. This is not substantiated either for ownership of various material items or for expenditure patterns on basic food, alcohol, and shelter items. This myth deserves to die a quick death.

Household Items by Income Group

Higher income households have more of everything that costs money.

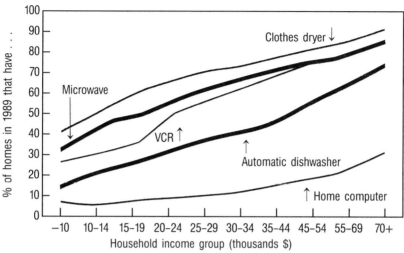

Author based on Statistics Canada, 13–216

Household Items by Age Group

Homes with the head aged 35 to 54 are most likely to be filled with modern gadgets.

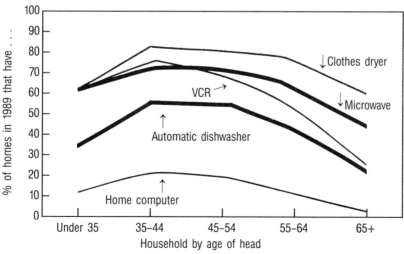

Author based on Statistics Canada, 13–216

141

People Pattern No. 57
Spending and the Age-Income Matrix

The previous examination of ownership patterns looked at how income affected ownership rates and then at how age affected ownership rates. The combination of both of these two key factors provides more insight than either factor considered alone.

Examining both income and age together is easy for individual households because we know the age of the head of our households and we know our incomes. The two examples discussed can be extended to many other ownership characteristics.

The age-income matrix for renters (top table) indicates that about 90 percent of householders who are less than 35 years of age and who earn under $10,000 of income are renters. As householders with incomes of $10,000 or less grow older, the percentage who are renters declines to 52 percent by the age of 55–64 and then rises again.

Only 26 percent of young householders with incomes of $70,000 and over are renters.

Based on this age-income matrix it is clear that those most likely to be renters are the youngest and poorest. Those least likely to be renters have an income of $70,000 and over and are 55–64 years of age. Of this latter group about 60 percent own a home without a mortgage.

The rate of VCR ownership (bottom table) rises sharply with income within each of the age groups. Peak ownership of VCRs is for households with heads aged 35–44 and incomes of $70,000 and over (87 percent). The lowest rate of VCR ownership is among householders with incomes of less than $10,000 and aged 65 and over.

The highest and lowest proportions of householders who own microwaves and home computers are in exactly the same cells as for VCRs.

And so what . . . The examination of purchasing patterns can be best appreciated through the use of the age-income matrix approach. Sophisticated marketers use this method to pinpoint those household groups which should be the focus of advertising for specific types of products and services.

Percentage of Households Within Each "Age-Income" Cell Who Are Renters

Only 7 percent of households headed by people ages 55 to 64 and with over $70,000 in annual income are renters.

Household Income Group	Age of Head of Household in 1989				
	Under 35	35–44	45–54	55–64	65+
Under $10,000	89	78	65	52	59
$10,000–14,999	87	70	50	42	48
$15,000–19,999	82	60	43	31	35
$20,000–24,999	74	47	43	29	27
$25,000–29,999	66	36	29	23	} 21
$30,000–34,999	60	28	26	23	
$35,000–44,999	50	26	23	19	21
$45,000–54,999	41	16	17	13	
$55,000–69,999	35	14	17	12	} 12
$70,000+	26	12	9	7	

Author based on Statistics Canada, 13–218

Percentage of Households Within Each "Age-Income" Cell With VCRs

The incidence of VCR ownership is highest—at 87 percent—in households with a head aged 35 to 44 and an annual income of $70,000 or more.

Household Income Group	Age of Head of Household in 1989				
	Under 35	35–44	45–54	55–64	65+
Under $10,000	34	43	26	28	14
$10,000–14,999	41	56	42	38	17
$15,000–19,999	44	59	53	31	21
$20,000–24,999	55	64	52	49	35
$25,000–29,999	59	69	60	52	} 35
$30,000–34,999	66	72	61	57	
$35,000–44,999	71	77	69	58	39
$45,000–54,999	77	84	77	67	
$55,000–69,999	81	85	79	62	} 55
$70,000+	79	87	84	77	

Author based on Statistics Canada, 13–218

A Future for George, Amanda, and You

R eaders have surely sensed that certain People Patterns are accurate descriptions of their changing lives. At other times, readers may have felt that the patterns reflect the lifestyles or circumstances of people they know.

The reality is that is each one of us is a very complex individual with unique characteristics. Much depends on where we started, where we are now, the circumstances that have come our way, and the choices we make in the future. We are different ages, are male or female, live in different sized families, live alone, are single, married, divorced, or widowed, have different levels of education, have large variations in incomes and wealth, and have different jobs.

The theoretical examples that follow serve to illustrate how possible futures for two individuals can be visualized based on the linkages between the various People Patterns presented in this book. Readers can also build more concrete scenarios to portray futures for themselves or for someone they know.

A Future for George

George has just celebrated his 44th birthday. He is married and has two children, who are in grades 10 and 12. His wife, Margaret, does not work outside the home. George got his high school diploma in 1964 and has experienced periods of employment followed by bouts of unemployment ever since. He was last unemployed for 25 weeks during the recession-depression of the early 1980s. He has made steady progress over the last seven years after joining a medium-sized manufacturing company in a medium-sized city. His income increased during this period but has still lagged behind the advance in the cost of living. He has a $50,000 mortgage on a house worth about $100,000 and has about $5,000 in savings.

For George, the ups and downs of the economy are always real. The recession that many economists have been forecasting finally arrives in 1994. Within a few months the Canadian unemployment rate rises from 8 percent to 12 percent. At the age of 48 George has lost his job again. He gets a few months of severance pay and begins to collect unemployment insurance.

George begins to look for another job. He quickly becomes aware that, in times of recession, a 48-year-old male typically takes about 7 to 8 months to find a job. He is viewed as inflexible and lacking in new skills. George has landed in a difficult situation and he has difficult choices to make.

George's understanding of the reality of the impacts of a recession helps him to make informed choices. He sits down with his family and they reach a consensus on a course of action. The family decides that (1) non-essential spending will be cut starting now, (2) Margaret will apply for a part-time job at the local fast-food outlet, which is opening in two weeks, (3) George will enrol in a community college to update his skills while looking for a job, and (4) they will ask George's mother to move in with them. They will dig into the $5,000 in savings and arrange to increase the size of their mortgage if and when the savings run out.

Margaret is lucky and lands her first paying job since getting married. She loves it. She gets a promotion within a matter of weeks and manages to make enough money to pay most of the monthly mortgage payment. The joys of working fit her style. Margaret now decides that she will return to school when George gets a job. The severance pay, unemployment insurance, the contribution from George's mother, and the savings are not quite enough to get by. The children get part-time jobs to pay their way through school and get student loans.

George finishes his course in 1995 and gets a better job than the one he had earlier. The recession finally ends. The family sets a course to build up their savings once again. The family becomes a double-income family for the long haul. They view it as a form of insurance.

In the year 2000, George turns 54. He is becoming aware of the labour shortage facing the Canadian economy. He, along with most other workers, starts to achieve real wage gains; the first real gains in almost 25 years. Employers are encouraging a large increase in immigration.

George turns 65 in 2011. He feels that his pension is not yet good enough to enable him to retire. The labour shortage is so severe that he is persuaded to work for another five years (until 2016) but on a part-time basis. Margaret decides to continue to work full-time and get full value out of her new university degree. George lives to the age of 76 and dies in 2022. Margaret sells her house since she suspects that housing prices will decline when the peak in household numbers is reached in about another decade. Margaret passes away in 2031 at the age of 84.

Was George's recovery from unemployment a fairy tale? It could be the happy reality. On the other hand, George could have lost his job again during the recession of 2002, have remained unemployed, broken up with Margaret, and by the year 2011 still be living in poverty like one-third of all unattached senior citizens.

A Future for Amanda

Amanda is now 17 years old and is about to graduate from high school. She has been raised in a family that has had sufficient income to supply the necessities of life and a little extra. Amanda's parents were part of that generation that felt the "real" income squeeze of the 1980s.

Luckily, Amanda has the capacity and desire to go to university. She obtains her university degree in 1995 with the knowledge that she has potentially added several thousands of dollars to her future annual income compared with the situation she would have experienced if she had entered the full-time job market in 1990.

Amanda's age (she is now 22) is a strong plus for her as the relative position of young people (aged 15–24) has been improving throughout the 1980s and so far in the 1990s, due to the declining number of youth. She will be in a relatively strong position all of her life because of the small number of individuals in her group and the smaller numbers that will follow her.

Around the year 2000, Amanda decides to remain childless for the rest of her life and to devote herself to her career and to self-fulfillment. Her common-law partner (they are thinking of getting married some day but are in no rush) has chosen to develop his consulting practice out of their home. His computer can be linked to any computer in the world. They consider themselves lucky that the number of gadgets available for household chores enable them to spend little time performing these chores.

Up until the age of 30 (about 2003) Amanda struggles for equality of pay and promotion with men. This disadvantage disappears when she is about 40 years old (about 2013) as the severe labour shortage takes hold.

When Amanda turns 50 (about 2023) she is overwhelmed by offers of senior executive positions as the last of the baby boomers retire. Amanda finds that taxes have been increasing rapidly to help support the retired baby boomers who have now gained strong political influence. The 65 and over now represent almost one-quarter of the Canadian population.

When Amanda turns 63 (in 2036) she finds that the younger work force is now very unsympathetic to the financial needs of the less fortunate in her age group. Those in the younger work force are feeling the strains caused by the rising dependency ratio. Amanda never did get married and is now living with her third common-law partner. Amanda's female friends complain that men their own age are hard to find.

Amanda has travelled extensively throughout her life and will continue to do so beyond 2036 . . . but that is another story.

And A Future For You . . .

List of Graphs

About the Author

Roger Sauvé is an economist, demographer, corporate planner and journalist who has studied Canadian households for over two decades. A former president of the Toronto Association of Business Economists, he holds an undergraduate degree in social sciences and a masters in economics.

In addition to running his own consulting firm and extensive work with credit unions and caisse populaires, Roger has worked for one of Canada's largest department stores, one of Canada's largest banks, Canada's largest farm co-operative, international oil and mining companies, and government.

Roger has addressed business and consumer organizations, including The Conference Board and The North American Planning Association, and is a popular seminar leader. He has published articles in *The Financial Post* and has served as a consumer and business columnist with prairie newspapers. He is a member of the Senior Business Economists Group, the Canadian Association for Business Economics, and the World Futures Society.